W9-AUI-694

At Issue

| Violent Video Games

Other Books in the At Issue Series:

At Issue

|Violent Video Games

Roman Espejo, Book Editor

GREENHAVEN PRESS
A part of Gale, Cengage Learning

GALE
CENGAGE Learning·

Farmington Hills, Mich • San Francisco • New York • Waterville, Maine
Meriden, Conn • Mason, Ohio • Chicago

Elizabeth Des Chenes, *Director, Content Strategy*
Douglas Dentino, *Manager, New Product*

For more information, contact:
Greenhaven Press
27500 Drake Rd.
Farmington Hills, MI 48331-3535
Or you can visit our Internet site at gale.cengage.com

For product information and technology assistance, contact us at

Gale Customer Support, 1-800-877-4253
For permission to use material from this text or product, submit all requests online at www.cengage.com/permissions

Further permissions questions can be e-mailed to permissionrequest@cengage.com

Articles in Greenhaven Press anthologies are often edited for length to meet page requirements. In addition, original titles of these works are changed to clearly present the main thesis and to explicitly indicate the author's opinion. Every effort is made to ensure that Greenhaven Press accurately reflects the original intent of the authors. Every effort has been made to trace the owners of copyrighted material.

Cover photograph reproduced by permission of Brand X Pictures.

LIBRARY OF CONGRESS CATALOGING-IN-PUBLICATION DATA

Violent video games / Roman Espejo, book editor.
    pages cm. -- (At issue)
    Includes bibliographical references and index.
    ISBN 978-0-7377-7195-4 (hardcover) -- ISBN 978-0-7377-7196-1 (pbk.)
    1. Video games and children. 2. Video games and teenagers. 3. Violence in video games. 4. Children and violence. 5. Youth and violence. I. Espejo, Roman, 1977-
    HQ784.V53V56 2015
    794.8083--dc23
                                                            2014021946

Printed in the United States of America
1 2 3 4 5 6 7 18 17 16 15 14

Contents

Introduction

While awarding 2013's *Grand Theft Auto V* a score of nine out of ten in a review, GameSpot staff writer Carolyn Petit criticized the latest in the blockbuster game series for its sexism. "GTA V has little room for women except to portray them as strippers, prostitutes, long-suffering wives, humorless girlfriends and goofy, new-age feminists we're meant to laugh at,"[1] says Petit. "Characters constantly spout lines that glorify male sexuality while demeaning women, and the billboards and radio stations of the world reinforce this misogyny, with ads that equate manhood with sleek sports cars while encouraging women to purchase a fragrance that will make them 'smell like a bitch,'" she adds. Explaining her position, Petit insists that the characterization and treatment of women in *Grand Theft Auto V* lack any meaningful context. "With nothing in the narrative to underscore how insane and wrong this is, all the game does is reinforce and celebrate sexism," she concludes.

As in television, movies, and music, misogyny is a recurring issue in video games. Released in 1982, *Custer's Revenge* attracted controversy for enabling the player to rape a Native American woman tied to a pole. The following decade, Lara Croft, the central heroine of the *Tomb Raider* series, sparked complaints that the buxom, scantily clad character was hypersexualized, especially for an archeologist. And more recently, *RapeLay*, a Japanese video game, was widely condemned for making play out of sexual assault. For instance, the player harasses and gropes a mother and her two daughters in a subway station, with the goal of arousing them despite their fearful reactions. "The physical character design can obviously be sexist—in fact, that's usually its entire job—but often it's the

---

1. Carolyn Petit, "City of Angels and Demons," GameSpot, September 16, 2013. http://www.gamespot.com/reviews/grand-theft-auto-v-review/1900-6414475.

narrative structures that wrap the player in a matrix of sexism,"[2] states Cracked, a humor and culture website.

To examine representations of women in video games, media critic and gamer Anita Sarkeesian created the multiepisode "Tropes vs. Women in Video Games" for her web series *Feminist Frequency*. "One of the reasons I decided to dedicate a series exclusively to video games is because the way women are represented in the medium is consistently abysmal,"[3] she maintains. The vast majority of female characters, Sarkeesian argues, are limited to sexist stereotypes and clichés, from helpless damsels in distress to sexually objectified sidekicks and villains. "Developers are perfectly willing to bend, twist or entirely throw out the laws of physics and no one bats an eye," asserts Sarkeesian, "but somehow it's impossible to imagine even an alternative reality in which most women aren't horribly oppressed, stereotyped or merely decorative." In her view, video games are a powerful and pervasive part of popular culture, and their distortions of gender must be addressed. "Think of it this way, if gaming is the air we all breathe, right now the air quality is currently extremely polluted with thick clouds of toxic sexism with radioactive particles of misogyny floating around everywhere."[4]

Not everyone, however, believes that video games and gaming suffer from an extreme level of sexism. "The poor treatment of women in video games is not because male gamers are, by and large, causatively sexist,"[5] contends Joe Yang, founder of Project Cognizance, an academic website on video games. Yang persists that the problem does not plague gaming

2. "6 Sexist Video Game Problems Even Bigger than the Breasts," Cracked, September 19, 2013. http://www.cracked.com/blog/6-sexist-video-game-problems-even-bigger -than-breasts.
3. Anita Sarkeesian, interviewed by Paul Dean, "Full IGN Interview with Anita Sarkeesian," Feminist Frequency, June 6, 2013. http://www.feministfrequency.com/2013/06 /full-ign-interview-with-anita-sarkeesian/#more-8129.
4. Ibid.
5. Joe Yang, "Why Gaming Culture Is Not Misogynistic," GamesBeat, December 11, 2012. http://venturebeat.com/2012/12/11/why-gaming-culture-is-not-misogynistic.

any more than other mediums of entertainment. "None of the issues regarding misogyny in the video game industry are unique, or even caused by the distinctive ritual behaviours that exist," he purports. On the contrary, Yang proposes that representations of women are evolving more rapidly toward equality in video games than in other media. "Video games, I would argue, are becoming progressive in [their] narrative much faster because as gender becomes more prevalent, the culture is providing more focus on a female perspective,"[6] claims Yang.

As for *Grand Theft Auto V*, Carolyn Petit's criticism of misogyny has been questioned. "Yes, overwhelmingly the game has a terribly negative portrayal of women. But I think we're missing the other side of the coin here,"[7] asserts Paul Tassi, a *Forbes* contributor covering video games and technology. "The game has a terribly negative portrayal of men too." Among these portrayals, he observes, include "lazy good-for-nothings," perverts, and racists. "All the side characters of both genders are crazy and one-dimensional in GTA 5," Tassi suggests. "The fact that there isn't a female lead means that there's really no chance for a female character to be both a ruthless killer and criminal like the guys, and likable as we learn more about her and find her redeeming qualities."

Grand Theft Auto V generated $1 billion in sales in a mere three days, so the next installment in the franchise is certain to keep to its formula of violence and antisocial themes and, perhaps, be more realistic. Outpacing the music industry worldwide, the whopping sales figure is also a reminder that the demand and popularity of violent video games show no signs of slowing down. *At Issue: Violent Video Games* explores their potential psychological, cognitive, and social impacts—both harmful and promising—on gamers.

---

6. Ibid.
7. Paul Tassi, "On Gender and 'GTA 5,'" *Forbes*, September 26, 2013. http://www.forbes.com/sites/insertcoin/2013/09/26/on-gender-and-gta-5.

1

Violent Video Games Can Benefit Children

Isabela Granic, Adam Lobel, and Rutger C.M.E. Engels

Isabela Granic, Adam Lobel, and Rutger C.M.E. Engels are scholars in the Developmental Psychopathology Department, Behavioral Science Institute, at Radboud University Nijmegen in the Netherlands.

Emerging research demonstrates that violent video games—which have become remarkably complex, realistic, and social—are beneficial in several ways as forms of play. Cognitively, gamers gain enhanced abilities in attention allocation, visual processing, and mental rotation—effects not documented in puzzle or role-playing games. Motivationally, gamers engage in play that balances challenge and frustration, which encourages success and achievement. As for the emotional benefits, they experience improved moods, positive feelings, and a strong sense of pride and control. And socially, gamers are not isolated but participate with others in so-called helping behaviors—even in violent video games that promote cooperation. Conclusively, video games can potentially serve as interventions that support wellbeing and mental health.

Today, in the United States, 91% of children between the ages of 2 and 17 play video games, and a nationally representative study of U.S. teenagers found that up to 99% of boys and 94% of girls play these games. In the United States alone,

Granic, I., Lobel, A., & Engels, R.C.M.E. (2014). "The Benefits of Playing Video Games," *American Psychologist*, 69(1), 66-78. doi:10.1037/a0034857. Copyright © 2014 by the American Psychological Association. Adapted with permission.

video games brought in over $25 billion in 2010, more than doubling Hollywood's 2010 box office sales of $10.8 billion in the United States and Canada. Against this backdrop of nearly ubiquitous play, the popular press regularly pulses out urgent warnings against the perils of addiction to these games and their inevitable link to violence and aggression, especially in children and adolescents. Indeed, the vast majority of psychological research on the effects of "gaming" has been focused on its negative impact: the potential harm related to aggression, addiction, and depression. It is likely that this focus will not diminish in the near future, in part because of the enormous media attention garnered when mass killings (e.g., the Columbine High School slayings in 1999) are associated with youth who play violent video games. Most recently, the revelation that the Sandy Hook Elementary School gunman played shooter games directly resulted in President Obama requesting Congress to allocate $10 million for research on the effects of violent media, especially video games.

A recent functional magnetic resonance imaging (fMRI) study found that ... shooter game players allocate their attentional resources more efficiently and filter out irrelevant information more effectively.

Decades of valuable research on the effects of violent video games on children's and adolescents' aggressive behavior already exists, and this is indeed an important body of work to consider. However, we argue that in order to understand the impact of video games on children's and adolescents' development, a more balanced perspective is needed, one that considers not only the possible negative effects but also the benefits of playing these games. Considering these potential benefits is important, in part, because the nature of these games has changed dramatically in the last decade, becoming increasingly complex, diverse, realistic and social in nature. A small but significant body of research has begun to emerge, mostly in the last five years, documenting these benefits. We propose that, taken together, these findings suggest that video games provide youth with immersive and compelling social, cognitive, and emotional experiences. Further, these experiences may have the potential to enhance mental health and well-being in children and adolescents.

In this article, we summarize the research on the benefits of playing video games, focusing on four main domains: cognitive (e.g., attention), motivational (e.g., resilience in the face of failure), emotional (e.g., mood management), and social (e.g., prosocial behavior) benefits. By integrating insights from developmental, positive, and social psychology, as well as media psychology, we propose some candidate mechanisms by which playing video games fosters real-world benefits. Our hope is to provide strong enough evidence and a theoretical rationale to inspire new programs of research on the largely unexplored mental health benefits of gaming. Finally, we end with a call to intervention and prevention researchers to test the potential positive uses of video games, and we suggest several promising directions for doing so. . . .

Cognitive Benefits of Gaming

Contrary to conventional beliefs that playing video games is intellectually lazy and sedating, it turns out that playing these games promotes a wide range of cognitive skills. This is particularly true for *shooter* video games (often called "action" games by researchers), many of which are violent in nature (e.g., *Halo 4, Grand Theft Auto IV*). The most convincing evidence comes from the numerous training studies that recruit naive gamers (those who have hardly or never played *shooter* video games) and randomly assign them to play either a shooter video game or another type of video game for the same period of time. Compared to control participants, those in the shooter video game condition show faster and more accurate attention allocation, higher spatial resolution in visual processing, and enhanced mental rotation abilities. A recently published meta-analysis concluded that the spatial skills improvements derived from playing commercially available shooter video games are comparable to the effects of formal (high school and university-level) courses aimed at enhancing these same skills. Further, this recent meta-analysis showed that spatial skills can be trained with video games in a relatively brief period, that these training benefits last over an extended period of time, and crucially, that these skills transfer to other spatial tasks outside the video game context.

These training studies have critical implications for education and career development. A 25-year longitudinal study with a U.S. representative sample established the power of spatial skills in predicting achievement in science, technology, engineering, and mathematics (STEM). STEM areas of expertise have been repeatedly linked to long-term career success and are predicted to be especially critical in the next century.

New evidence is emerging that playing any kind of video game, regardless of whether or not it is violent, enhances children's creative capacities.

Preliminary research has also demonstrated that these cognitive advantages manifest in measurable changes in neural processing and efficiency. For example, a recent functional magnetic resonance imaging (fMRI) study found that the mechanisms that control attention allocation (e.g., the fronto-parietal network) were less active during a challenging pattern-detection task in regular gamers than in nongamers, leading the researchers to suggest that shooter game players allocate their attentional resources more efficiently and filter out irrelevant information more effectively. As summarized recently in *Nature Reviews Neuroscience*: "Video games are controlled training regimens delivered in highly motivating behavioral contexts . . . because behavioral changes arise from brain changes, it is also no surprise that performance improvements are paralleled by enduring physical and functional neurological remodeling." These changes in neural functioning may be one means by which the cognitive skills gained through video games generalize to contexts outside games.

Visually Rich and Fast-Paced

It is important to stress that enhanced cognitive performance is not documented for all video game genres. The most robust effects on cognitive performance come from playing shooter video games and not from, for example, *puzzle* or *role-playing* games. These cognitive enhancements are likely a product of the visually rich three-dimensional navigational spaces and the fast-paced demands that require split-second decision making and acute attention to unpredictable changes in context. These assumptions, however, remain somewhat speculative because the vast majority of video games include an enormous number of game mechanics intertwined, rendering specific hypothesis testing about these mechanisms extremely difficult. Moreover, it is virtually impossible to choose an appropriate control condition wherein all aspects of a game (e.g., visual stimulation, arousal induction, gameplay) are kept constant across conditions and only one cognitive challenge is manipulated (e.g., navigating three-dimensional space efficiently vs. inhibiting pre-potent responses). Cognitive neuroscientists have just recently put out a call to game developers to design new games for testing hypotheses about the specificity of cognitive advances and the particular mechanisms on which they are based.

In addition to spatial skills, scholars have also speculated that video games are an excellent means for developing problem-solving skills. Indeed, problem solving seems central to all genres of video games (including those with violent content). In-game puzzles range in complexity from finding the quickest route from A to B, to discovering complex action sequences based on memorization and analytical skills. Further, game designers often provide very little instruction about how to solve in-game problems, providing players with a nearly blank palette from which to explore a huge range of possible solutions based on past experience and intuitions. . . .

Finally, video games seem to be associated with an additional cognitive benefit: enhanced creativity. New evidence is emerging that playing any kind of video game, regardless of whether or not it is violent, enhances children's creative capacities. For example, among a sample of almost 500 12-year-old students, video game playing was positively associated with creativity. Critically, children's use of other forms of technology (e.g., computer, Internet, cell phone) did not relate to enhanced creativity. However, this study's cross-sectional design made it unclear whether playing video games develops creative skills or creative people prefer video games (or both). . . .

Motivational Benefits of Gaming

Game designers are wizards of engagement. They have mastered the art of pulling people of all ages into virtual environments, having them work toward meaningful goals, persevere in the face of multiple failures, and celebrate the rare moments of triumph after successfully completing challenging tasks. In this section, we do not focus on the motivations children and youth have for playing video games. Instead, we aim to identify several characteristics of video games that seem to promote an effective motivational style both in and outside gaming contexts. Specifically, decades of research in developmental and educational psychology suggest that motivational styles characterized by persistence and continuous effortful engagement are key contributors to success and achievement.

According to [researcher C.S.] Dweck and her colleagues, children develop beliefs about their intelligence and abilities, beliefs that underlie specific motivational styles and directly affect achievement. Children who are praised for their traits rather than their efforts (e.g., "Wow, you're such a smart boy") develop an *entity* theory of intelligence, which maintains that intelligence is an innate trait, something that is fixed and cannot be improved. In contrast, children who are praised for their effort (e.g., "You worked so hard on that puzzle!") develop an *incremental* theory of intelligence; they believe intelligence is malleable, something that can be cultivated through effort and time. We propose that video games are an ideal training ground for acquiring an incremental theory of intelligence because they provide players concrete, immediate feedback regarding specific *efforts* players have made.

We propose that being immersed in these gaming environments teaches players an essential basic lesson: Persistence in the face of failure reaps valued rewards.

The "Sweet Spot"

Immediate and concrete feedback in video games (e.g., through points, coins, dead ends in puzzles) serves to reward continual effort and keep players within what [researcher L.] Vygotsky coined the "zone of proximal development." This motivational "sweet spot" balances optimal levels of challenge and frustration with sufficient experiences of success and accomplishment. Importantly, in the best games available on the market, this "sweet spot" is so effective because it adjusts itself dynamically; the difficulty level is continuously being calibrated to players' abilities through increasingly more difficult puzzles demanding more dexterity, quicker reaction times, and more clever and complex solutions.

Further, research has shown that the extent to which individuals endorse an incremental versus entity theory of intelligence reliably predicts whether individuals in challenging circumstances will persist or give up, respectively. Thus, these implicit theories of intelligence have implications for how failure is processed and dealt with. If one believes that intelligence or ability is fixed, failure induces feelings of worthlessness. But if intelligence or ability is presumed to be a mark of effortful engagement, failure signals the need to remain engaged and bolster one's efforts. In turn, this positive attitude toward failure predicts better academic performance.

Notably, video games use failure as motivational tools and provide only intermittent chances for large-scale success. As behaviorists have documented for decades, the kinds of intermittent reinforcement schedules that are doled out to video game players are the most effective for "training" new behaviors. We propose that being immersed in these gaming environments teaches players an essential basic lesson: Persistence in the face of failure reaps valued rewards. Moreover, contrary to what we might expect, these experiences of failure do not lead to anger, frustration, or sadness, although players often do feel these negative emotions intermittently. Instead, or as well, players respond to failures with excitement, interest, and joy. When faced with failure, players are highly motivated to return to the task of winning, and they are "relentlessly optimistic" about reaching their goals. The development of a persistent motivational style charged with positive affect may, in turn, lead to lasting educational success. . . .

Emotional Benefits of Gaming

Based on the uses and gratifications theory, one of the oldest and most well-validated theories in communications research, among the top reasons individuals cite for using diverse forms of media are to manage their moods and to enhance their emotional states. Gaming may be among the most efficient and effective means by which children and youth generate positive feelings. Several studies have shown a causal relation between playing preferred video games and improved mood or increases in positive emotion. For example, studies suggest that playing *puzzle* video games—games with minimal interfaces, short-term commitments, and a high degree of accessibility (e.g., *Angry Birds, Bejewled II)*—can improve players' moods, promote relaxation, and ward off anxiety.

It has further been suggested that some of the most intense positive emotional experiences are triggered in the context of playing video games. For instance, *fiero,* the Italian word for intense pride after succeeding against great adversity, is a feeling that gamers often report seeking and experiencing. *Flow* or *transportation* is another positive emotional experience described by gamers, during which they are immersed in an intrinsically rewarding activity that elicits a high sense of control while simultaneously evoking a loss of self-consciousness. In psychology, flow experiences have repeatedly been linked to a host of positive outcomes for adolescents, including commitment and achievement in high school, higher self-esteem, and less anxiety. Experiencing flow or transportation in games may lead to similar positive real-world outcomes; however, this hypothesis remains untested.

> *Contrary to stereotypes, the average gamer is not a socially isolated, inept nerd who spends most of his (or her) time alone loafing on the couch.*

Although not specific to game playing, the importance of experiencing positive emotions on a daily basis has been elaborated in [researcher B.L.] Fredrickson's broaden-and-build theory of positive emotions. She demonstrates that experiencing positive emotions may help *broaden* the number of behaviors one perceives as both possible and motivating and may *build* social relationships that provide support for goal pursuit and coping with failure. Further, Fredrickson and colleagues propose that positive emotions help undo the detrimental and de-motivating results of negative emotions. Positive emotions are thus the bedrock for well-being, crucial not only as end states but as sources of inspiration and connectivity. If playing games simply makes people happier, this seems to be a fundamental emotional benefit to consider. . . .

Evaluating the emotional benefits of video games leads to the study of emotion regulation in these contexts. Simple up-regulation of positive emotions is one emotion-regulation strategy that has been linked to beneficial outcomes, but there may be additional emotion-regulation benefits of playing video games. Games do not elicit only positive emotions; video games also trigger a range of negative ones, including frustration, anger, anxiety, and sadness. But similar to what [researcher J.M.] Gottman's research has shown on the function of traditional play, the pretend context of video games may be real enough to make the accomplishment of goals matter but also safe enough to practice controlling, or modulating, negative emotions in the service of those goals. Adaptive regulation strategies such as acceptance, problem solving, and reappraisal have repeatedly been linked to less negative affect, more social support, and lower levels of depressive symptoms. These same adaptive regulation strategies seem to be rewarded in gaming contexts because their use is concretely and clearly linked to goal achievement. . . .

Social Benefits of Gaming

Perhaps the biggest difference in the characteristics of video games today, compared to their predecessors of 10 to 20 years ago, is their pervasive social nature. Contrary to stereotypes, the average gamer is not a socially isolated, inept nerd who spends most of his (or her) time alone loafing on the couch. Over 70% of gamers play their games with a friend, either cooperatively or competitively. For example, *World of Warcraft*—a multiplayer fantasy game set in a massive virtual world—boasts 12 million regular players, and *Farmville*—one of the most popular social networking games on Facebook—

hosted over 5 million daily users in 2012. In these virtual social communities, decisions need to be made on the fly about whom to trust, whom to reject, and how to most effectively lead a group. Given these immersive social contexts, we propose that gamers are rapidly learning social skills and prosocial behavior that might generalize to their peer and family relations outside the gaming environment.

Players seem to acquire important prosocial skills when they play games that are specifically designed to reward effective cooperation, support, and helping behaviors. One study that summarized international evidence from correlational, longitudinal, and experimental studies found that playing prosocial video games consistently related to, or predicted, prosocial behaviors. More specifically, playing prosocial games led to causal, short-term effects on "helping" behaviors, and longitudinal effects were also found, in that children who played more prosocial games at the beginning of the school year were more likely to exhibit helpful behaviors later that year. It may be tempting to conclude from this work that games with exclusively nonviolent, prosocial content lead to prosocial behavior. But compelling work is just emerging that seems to refute this simple interpretation, suggesting that violent games are just as likely to promote prosocial behavior. The critical dimension that seems to determine whether violent games are associated with helping, prosocial behavior versus malevolent, antisocial behavior is the extent to which they are played cooperatively versus competitively. For example, players who play violent games that encourage cooperative play are more likely to exhibit helpful gaming behaviors online and offline than those who play nonviolent games, and playing violent video games socially (in groups) reduces feelings of hostility compared with playing alone. Likewise, violent video games played cooperatively seem to decrease players' access to aggressive cognitions. Two recent studies have also shown that playing a violent video game cooperatively, compared with competitively, increases subsequent prosocial, co-operative behavior outside of the game context and can even overcome the effects of outgroup membership status (making players more cooperative with outgroup members than if they had played competitively...). Conversely, recently published experimental studies suggest that even the most violent video games on the market (*Grand Theft Auto IV, Call of Duty*) fail to diminish subsequent prosocial behavior. All of these studies examined immediate, short-term effects of cooperative play, but they point to potential long-term benefits as well. The social benefits of cooperative versus competitive game play need to be studied longitudinally, with repeated assessments, to have clearer implications for policy and practice. . . .

The Inspiring Potential of Games

After pulling together the research findings on the benefits of video games, we have become particularly inspired by the potential that these games hold for interventions that promote well-being, including the prevention and treatment of mental health problems in youth. Remarkably, there are very few video games that have been developed with these aims in mind. Given how enthralled most children and adolescents are with video games, we believe that a multidisciplinary team of psychologists, clinicians, and game designers can work together to develop genuinely innovative approaches to mental health interventions.

2

Violent Video Games Can Desensitize Players and Increase Aggression

George Drinka

George Drinka is a psychiatrist for children and adolescents. He is the author of the book When the Media Is the Parent.

It is probable that mass murderers—engaging in isolated, prolonged play—have used violent video games to train themselves to kill. Experts note that playing them improves eye-hand coordination for efficiently aiming and firing a gun. More importantly, numerous studies suggest that these games desensitize players to the pain of others. A recent article finds that during such play, brain activity associated with empathy is suppressed, and another proposes that twenty minutes of playing violent video games for three consecutive days lowered empathy and increased aggression in children. It is plausible to conjecture that for mass murderers, their rage and the violent fantasy of video games lead to planned shootings in real life.

At the risk of being premature, I think enough material has now accrued for me to ask certain questions and offer specific conjectures about the inner life of [school shooter] Adam Lanza in the days and even minutes leading up to the Newtown shootings.

As is already known, for many years before the killing spree, Lanza's peers and neighbors perceived him as a peculiar, socially withdrawn adolescent. His brother has reported that he suffered from either autism or Asperger's syndrome, conditions highlighted by an inability to read the social cues of others, a problem that may explain his painful social isolation. School acquaintances recall instances of his eerily sidling backward along school corridor walls whenever they tried to approach him, a behavior suggesting significant fear and even paranoia. For a time he may have been home schooled, a way of life that only isolated him further from his peers. Not surprisingly, once high school ended, he became even more socially withdrawn.

Finally, and perhaps most crucially, at least one report describes the twenty-year-old holing up for hour upon hour in a basement area inside his home, outfitted with computers and a TV. This windowless space contained a bathroom and bed as well as a locked cupboard filled with guns, and its walls were plastered with posters of weaponry from the 1940s onward. There it seems he hid out for hours on end, solely engaged with the computers and the television.

> The common thread running through all of these games is that [the] player becomes the shooter, from whose vantage point behind the gun the player sees the world.

The police also describe discovering a vast cache of video games, many with violent content, in particular the game entitled *Call of Duty*. Since Anders Brevig, the Norwegian mass murderer, claimed he practiced for his mass shooting by playing this same game, many have already wondered about this seeming coincidence. Was this simply a fluke or not?

When the first version of *Call of Duty* initially became available in 2003, it soon became wildly popular. Due to high sales, its creators generated numerous sequels, and these games continue to fly off the shelves into the hands of eager kids and adults—such as Lanza—to this day.

In *Call of Duty 1, 2,* and *3,* the player takes on the identity of a fighter in World War II battles. Inserted into the British, US, and Russian armies, he goes toe-to-toe, battlefield to battlefield, house to house against the Nazis.

He dons the persona of soldiers in the three armies, and often spends multiple hours gunning down Nazis in cold blood with weaponry from the era. In more recent iterations of the game, the enthusiast becomes a CIA [Central Intelligence Agency] agent, a Special Forces fighter, or a black op. In these, he engages in shoot-outs around the world during the Cold War, then hurtles forward into present wars and beyond into a distant realm of 2028, where he fights zombies attempting to take over the planet.

The Player Becomes the Shooter

The common thread running through all of these games is that that player becomes the shooter, from whose vantage point behind the gun the player sees the world. The player points his weapon at his enemies and learns to pull the trigger with ever greater efficiency. Often he uses an automatic rifle with numerous rounds of ammo in every cartridge case. The enemies are always dehumanized—Nazis, Vietcong, zombies— and the shooter perfects the techniques of pointing accurately, squeezing the trigger smoothly, and moving on to the next victim.

To be sure, thousands of young people in this world, most of them male, have played these games for hours on end, and few have gone on killing crusades. Yet only a few, I suggest, have sequestered themselves in windowless rooms in basements and, cutting themselves off from most human contact, have played these games for such unending marathon sessions as Lanza seems to have done.

It is likely then, given how utterly he was secluded from the outer world, that the imagery of these games had become deeply imbedded in his memory and his psyche. In addition to this probability, we know through his acquaintances that Lanza was especially fond of using an automatic rifle for honing in on his prey. . . .

Desensitized to Actual Pain

Is it accurate to say that Lanza had become a computer game addict? Since he destroyed his computer just before he began the shootings, we may never know precisely what his video-gaming habits had become. Yet it does seem fair to say that he was an avid gamer, one who had few friends in real life and relied on these games for connection to the outer world—if the world within a video game can truly be likened to the outside world at all. And he probably, like Brevig, was training himself for the murders using these video games in the weeks and days leading up to the event.

[Researchers] found that the more days in a row the children played [violent games], the less empathy they manifested, and the more likely they were to demonstrate aggression in a laboratory setting.

How can I posit this? As experts in the field of the effects of violent video games on children have noted, playing video games does improve one's eye-hand coordination for other actions such as opening a soda can, handling a camera, or sadly, shooting real human beings with a gun in a theatre (as in Aurora), or at a youth camp (as in Brevig's case), or in a school. So video game training is in fact actual training when it comes to the acts of aiming and pulling a trigger as efficiently as possible, then moving on to one's next adversary.

But more important, as suggested by numerous scientific studies, playing violent video games desensitizes the player to actual pain suffered by others. And a very recent scholarly article pushed the matter even further, documenting via EEG [electroencephalography] apparatus connected to the players' skulls that in a certain part of the CNS (the locus-coeruleus norepinephrine system to be exact), activity becomes suppressed when these youths are playing violent games but not while playing nonviolent ones. This system of the brain is also implicated in eliciting empathy in humans. So with this portion of the brain's activity suppressed, the violent, video-game-playing human is shown to be less likely, per the same study, to feel empathy for any who suffer, including his own victims. In a word, he has become desensitized to the pain of others.

This study and others demonstrate this loss of sensitivity to the feelings of others via researchers in a laboratory setting, giving the youths involved an opportunity to hurt others with blaring noises that will potentially hurt their ear drums. We can extrapolate from this that Lanza was similarly working to desensitize himself for other, more sinister purposes. Either wittingly or otherwise, he set out to diminish his own sense of empathy for a time when he would later be pulling the trigger of a real gun in the classroom at Sandy Hook.

In another recent article, the researchers in a laboratory setting induced kids to play violent video games for only twenty minutes per day but for three consecutive days. They found that the more days in a row the children played, the less empathy they manifested, and the more likely they were to demonstrate aggression in a laboratory setting.

Isolated, Trapped, and Fuming with Rage

Where does this leave us with Lanza? We find a young man already socially isolated, perhaps in the early phase of a paranoid disorder, spending his days hiding in a basement room and incessantly playing video games, quite possibly for more than three days in a row, and most likely for more than twenty minutes per day.

How was he playing the game, solo or with others? As a few of my patients have clarified, one can play these games on Xbox live with others. At times these fellow players can be foul, sexist, hostile and violent in their language. Could they have egged him on toward actual violence? Or simply heightened his own sense of taking pleasure in killing? Or encouraged his own anger?

Though my conjectures may never be clarified due to his destroying his computer, we know that what little social surround still existing for him was collapsing at the time of the murders. His parents had divorced a few years earlier, and in retaliation, he cut off all contact with his dad once he'd remarried, and with his brother a year earlier. We find a boy with no friends, except perhaps a few "friends" made through his game playing, living alone with a mother who relates to him by giving him shooting lessons.

At least per newspaper reports, the mother feels she needs to continuously keep him near her in order to cope with his anger. She is also working on plans to disrupt his secluded life and move him to the West Coast, either to enter college or a therapeutic school. In short, we find a young man isolated, trapped, and fuming with rage over a variety of hurts and fears.

Fantasy Play Spills into Reality

In the same room where he plays the violent games stands a cupboard padlocked and brimming with real guns, including an automatic rifle. Per his mother's unwitting assistance, he has transferred some of his skills culled from playing video games into real life via shooting experience.

Not surprisingly, fantasy play spills into reality, and anger begets violence. Though first contained within the confines of game playing, his swirling wrath mingles with imagery of violent fantasy, and ultimately leads to his conjuring up a plan—

not unlike one of his black ops figures in *Call of Duty*, or Brevig in Norway—to go on a binge of mass destruction himself.

The plot unfolds with his first two victims, his mother in her bed receiving four bullets to the face, followed by his own computer, which had played the role of a mentor, a trainer, on his soon-to-be-enacted killing spree. The question remains: was he simply trying to destroy evidence when he riddled the computer with bullets, or was he actually enraged at the games themselves and his fellow players "met" via his gaming, for how they'd affected him?

3

Violent Video Games Do Not Cause Violence

Eric Kain

Eric Kain covers politics at the League of Ordinary Gentlemen, *a politics and culture blog, and writes about technology and video games for* Forbes.

Following recent mass shootings, condemnations and questions about violent video games and gun violence have reemerged. However, the truth does not match the rhetoric and moral panic. Research on causal and correlational links between game playing and aggression is inconsistent. Furthermore, America's consumption of violent video games is comparable to other industrialized nations with significantly fewer gun deaths. While some mass shooters have histories with violent video games, their gender and age group fits the target demographic and have high rates of mental illness. Such evidence also ignores the millions of players who do not kill. Therefore, public policy and research must focus on other possible causes of gun violence, such as poor mental health care and access to firearms, in addition to violent video games.

It was one of the most brutal video games imaginable—players used cars to murder people in broad daylight. Parents were outraged, and behavioral experts warned of real-world carnage. "In this game a player takes the first step to creating violence," a psychologist from the National Safety Council told the *New York Times*. "And I shudder to think what will come next if this is encouraged. It'll be pretty gory."

To earn points, *Death Race* encouraged players to mow down pedestrians. Given that it was 1976, those pedestrians were little pixel-gremlins in a 2-D black-and-white universe that bore almost no recognizable likeness to real people.

Indeed, the debate about whether violent video games lead to violent acts by those who play them goes way back. The public reaction to *Death Race* can be seen as an early predecessor to the controversial *Grand Theft Auto* three decades later and the many other graphically violent and hyper-real games of today, including the slew of new titles debuting at the E3 gaming summit this week in Los Angeles.

In the wake of the Newtown massacre and numerous other recent mass shootings, familiar condemnations of and questions about these games have reemerged. Here are some answers.

Amid a flurry of broader legislative activity on gun violence since Newtown there have been proposals specifically focused on video games.

Who's Claiming Video Games Cause Violence in the Real World?

Though conservatives tend to raise it more frequently, this bogeyman plays across the political spectrum, with regular calls for more research, more regulations, and more censorship. The tragedy in Newtown set off a fresh wave:

[Entrepreneur] Donald Trump tweeted: "Video game violence & glorification must be stopped—it's creating monsters!" [Political activist] Ralph Nader likened violent video games to "electronic child molesters." (His outlandish rhetoric was meant to suggest that parents need to be involved in the media their kids consume.) MSNBC's Joe Scarborough asserted that the government has a right to regulate video games, despite a Supreme Court ruling to the contrary.

Unsurprisingly, the most over-the-top talk came from the National Rifle Association:

"Guns don't kill people. Video games, the media, and Obama's budget kill people," NRA Executive Vice President Wayne LaPierre said at a press conference one week after the mass shooting at Sandy Hook Elementary. He continued without irony: "There exists in this country, sadly, a callous, corrupt and corrupting shadow industry that sells and stows violence against its own people through vicious, violent video games with names like *Bulletstorm, Grand Theft Auto, Mortal Kombat,* and *Splatterhouse.*"

Has the Rhetoric Led to Any Government Action?

Yes. Amid a flurry of broader legislative activity on gun violence since Newtown there have been proposals specifically focused on video games. Among them:

State Rep. Diane Franklin, a Republican in Missouri, sponsored a state bill that would impose a 1 percent tax on violent games, the revenues of which would go toward "the treatment of mental-health conditions associated with exposure to violent video games." (The bill has since been withdrawn.) Vice President Joe Biden has also promoted this idea.

Rep. Jim Matheson (D-Utah) proposed a federal bill that would give the Entertainment Software Rating Board's ratings system the weight of the law, making it illegal to sell Mature-rated games to minors, something Gov. Chris Christie (R-N.J.) has also proposed for his home state.

A bill introduced in the Senate by Sen. Jay Rockefeller (D-W.Va.) proposed studying the impact of violent video games on children.

So Who Actually Plays These Games and How Popular Are They?

While many of the top selling games in history have been various Mario and Pokemon titles, games from the the first-person-shooter genre, which appeal in particular to teen boys and young men, are also huge sellers.

The new king of the hill is Activision's *Call of Duty: Black Ops II*, which surpassed Wii Play as the No. 1 grossing game in 2012. *Call of Duty* is now one of the most successful franchises in video game history, topping charts year over year and boasting around 40 million active monthly users playing one of the franchise's games over the internet. (Which doesn't even include people playing the game offline.) There is already much anticipation for the release later this year [in 2013] of *Call of Duty: Ghosts*.

The *Battlefield* games from Electronic Arts also sell millions of units with each release. Irrational Games' *BioShock Infinite*, released in March, has sold nearly 4 million units and is one of the most violent games to date.

What Research Has Been Done on the Link Between Video Games and Violence, and What Does It Really Tell Us?

Studies on how violent video games affect behavior date to the mid 1980s, with conflicting results. Since then there have been at least two dozen studies conducted on the subject.

"Video Games, Television, and Aggression in Teenagers," published by the University of Georgia in 1984, found that playing arcade games was linked to increases in physical aggression. But a study published a year later by the Albert Einstein College of Medicine, "Personality, Psychopathology, and Developmental Issues in Male Adolescent Video Game Use," found that arcade games have a "calming effect" and that boys use them to blow off steam. Both studies relied on surveys and interviews asking boys and young men about their media consumption.

Games aren't developed in a vacuum, and they reflect the cultural milieu that produces them. So of course we have violent games.

Studies grew more sophisticated over the years, but their findings continued to point in different directions. A 2011 study found that people who had played competitive games, regardless of whether they were violent or not, exhibited increased aggression. In 2012, a different study found that cooperative playing in the graphically violent *Halo II* made the test subjects more cooperative even outside of video game playing.

Metastudies—comparing the results and the methodologies of prior research on the subject—have also been problematic. One published in 2010 by the American Psychological Association, analyzing data from multiple studies and more than 130,000 subjects, concluded that "violent video games increase aggressive thoughts, angry feelings, and aggressive behaviors and decrease empathic feelings and pro-social behaviors." But results from another metastudy showed that most studies of violent video games over the years suffered from publication biases that tilted the results toward foregone correlative conclusions.

Why Is It So Hard to Get Good Research on This Subject?

"I think that the discussion of media forms—particularly games—as some kind of serious social problem is often an attempt to kind of corral and solve what is a much broader social issue," says Carly Kocurek, a professor of Digital Humanities at the Illinois Institute of Technology. "Games aren't developed in a vacuum, and they reflect the cultural milieu that produces them. So of course we have violent games."

There is also the fundamental problem of measuring violent outcomes ethically and effectively.

"I think anybody who tells you that there's any kind of consistency to the aggression research is lying to you," Christopher J. Ferguson, associate professor of psychology and criminal justice at Texas A&M International University, told *Kotaku*. "There's no consistency in the aggression literature, and my impression is that at this point it is not strong enough to draw any kind of causal, or even really correlational links between video game violence and aggression, no matter how weakly we may define aggression."

Moreover, determining why somebody carries out a violent act like a school shooting can be very complex; underlying mental-health issues are almost always present. More than half of mass shooters over the last 30 years had mental-health problems.

But America's Consumption of Violent Video Games Must Help Explain Our Inordinate Rate of Gun Violence, Right?

Actually, no. A look at global video game spending per capita in relation to gun death statistics reveals that gun deaths in the United States far outpace those in other countries—including countries with higher per capita video game spending.

A 10-country comparison from the *Washington Post* shows the United States as the clear outlier in this regard. Countries with the highest per capita spending on video games, such as the Netherlands and South Korea, are among the safest countries in the world when it comes to guns. In other words, America plays about the same number of violent video games per capita as the rest of the industrialized world, despite that we far outpace every other nation in terms of gun deaths.

Or, consider it this way: With violent video game sales almost always at the top of the charts, why do so few gamers turn into homicidal shooters? In fact, the number of violent youth offenders in the United States fell by more than half between 1994 and 2010—while video game sales more than doubled since 1996. A working paper from economists on violence and video game sales published in 2011 found that higher rates of violent video game sales in fact correlated with a decrease in crimes, especially violent crimes.

I'm Still Not Convinced—A Bunch of Mass Shooters Were Gamers, Right?

Some mass shooters over the last couple of decades have had a history with violent video games. The Newtown shooter, Adam Lanza, was reportedly "obsessed" with video games. Norway shooter Anders Behring Breivik was said to have played *World of Warcraft* for 16 hours a day until he gave up the game in favor of *Call of Duty: Modern Warfare*, which he claimed he used to train with a rifle. Aurora theater shooter James Holmes was reportedly a fan of violent video games and movies such as *The Dark Knight*. (Holmes reportedly went so far as to mimic the Joker by dying his hair prior to carrying out his attack.)

To hold up a few sensational examples as causal evidence between violent games and violent acts ignores the millions of other young men and women who play violent video games and never go on a shooting spree in real life.

Jerald Block, a researcher and psychiatrist in Portland, Oregon, stirred controversy when he concluded that Columbine shooters Eric Harris and Dylan Klebold carried out their rampage after their parents took away their video games. According to the *Denver Post*, Block said that the two had relied on the virtual world of computer games to express their rage, and that cutting them off in 1998 had sent them into crisis.

But that's clearly an oversimplification. The age and gender of many mass shooters, including Columbine's, places them right in the target demographic for first-person-shooter (and most other) video games. And people between ages 18 and 25 also tend to report the highest rates of mental-health issues. Harris and Klebold's complex mental-health problems have been well documented.

To hold up a few sensational examples as causal evidence between violent games and violent acts ignores the millions of other young men and women who play violent video games and never go on a shooting spree in real life. Furthermore, it's very difficult to determine empirically whether violent kids are simply drawn to violent forms of entertainment, or if the entertainment somehow makes them violent. Without solid scientific data to go on, it's easier to draw conclusions that confirm our own biases.

How Is the Industry Reacting to the Latest Outcry over Violent Games?

Moral panic over the effects of violent video games on young people has had an impact on the industry over the years, says Kocurek, noting that "public and government pressure has driven the industry's efforts to self regulate."

In fact, it is among the best when it comes to abiding by its own voluntary ratings system, with self-regulated retail sales of Mature-rated games to minors lower than in any other entertainment field. . . .

But Is That Enough? Even Conservative Judges Think There Should Be Stronger Laws Regulating These Games, Right?

There have been two major Supreme Court cases involving video games and attempts by the state to regulate access to video games. *Aladdin's Castle, Inc. v. City of Mesquite* in 1983 and *Brown v. Entertainment Merchants Association* in 2011.

"Both cases addressed attempts to regulate youth access to games, and in both cases, the court held that youth access can't be curtailed," Kocurek says.

Violent video games are an easy thing to blame for a more complex problem.

In *Brown v. EMA*, the Supreme Court found that the research simply wasn't compelling enough to spark government action, and that video games, like books and film, were protected by the First Amendment.

"Parents who care about the matter can readily evaluate the games their children bring home," Justice Antonin Scalia wrote when the Supreme Court deemed California's video game censorship bill unconstitutional in *Brown v. EMA*. "Filling the remaining modest gap in concerned-parents' control can hardly be a compelling state interest."

So How Can We Explain the Violent Acts of Some Kids Who Play These Games?

For her part, Kocurek wonders if the focus on video games is mostly a distraction from more important issues. "When we talk about violent games," she says, "we are too often talking about something else and looking for a scapegoat."

In other words, violent video games are an easy thing to blame for a more complex problem. Public policy debates, she says, need to focus on serious research into the myriad factors that may contribute to gun violence. This may include video games—but a serious debate needs to look at the dearth of mental-health care in America, our abundance of easily accessible weapons, our highly flawed background-check system, and other factors.

There is at least one practical approach to violent video games, however, that most people would agree on: Parents should think deliberately about purchasing these games for their kids. Better still, they should be involved in the games their kids play as much as possible so that they can know firsthand whether the actions and images they're allowing their children to consume are appropriate or not.

4

Shooting in the Dark

Benedict Carey

Benedict Carey is a science reporter at The New York Times.

The mass shooters of Columbine High School, the movie theater in Colorado, and others seemingly acted out the violent fantasies of the video games they played. Nonetheless, new research reveals that while video games can heighten hostile urges and aggressive behaviors in players in the short term, it is unclear if such exposure increases the likelihood of someone committing a violent crime. Also, violent media is only one of several factors involved in shooting rampages, such as bullying, family problems, and mood disorders. Researchers, furthermore, have found that when violent video game sales increase, crime rates decrease. One theory is that games keep people off the street; another theory is that they provide an "outlet" for violent impulses.

The young men who opened fire at Columbine High School, at the movie theater in Aurora, Colo., and in other massacres had this in common: they were video gamers who seemed to be acting out some dark digital fantasy. It was as if all that exposure to computerized violence gave them the idea to go on a rampage—or at least fueled their urges.

But did it really?

Social scientists have been studying and debating the effects of media violence on behavior since the 1950s, and video games in particular since the 1980s. The issue is especially relevant today, because the games are more realistic and bloodier than ever, and because most American boys play them at some point. Girls play at lower rates and are significantly less likely to play violent games.

A burst of new research has begun to clarify what can and cannot be said about the effects of violent gaming. Playing the games can and does stir hostile urges and mildly aggressive behavior in the short term. Moreover, youngsters who develop a gaming habit can become slightly more aggressive—as measured by clashes with peers, for instance—at least over a period of a year or two.

Yet it is not at all clear whether, over longer periods, such a habit increases the likelihood that a person will commit a violent crime, like murder, rape, or assault, much less a Newtown-like massacre. (Such calculated rampages are too rare to study in any rigorous way, researchers agree.)

"I don't know that a psychological study can ever answer that question definitively," said Michael R. Ward, an economist at the University of Texas, Arlington. "We are left to glean what we can from the data and research on video game use that we have."

A dose of violent gaming makes people act a little more rudely than they would otherwise, at least for a few minutes after playing.

Three Categories of Research

The research falls into three categories: short-term laboratory experiments; longer-term studies, often based in schools; and correlation studies—between playing time and aggression, for instance, or between video game sales and trends in violent crime.

Lab experiments confirm what any gamer knows in his gut: playing games like "Call of Duty," "Killzone 3" or "Battlefield 3" stirs the blood. In one recent study, Christopher Barlett, a psychologist at Iowa State University, led a research team that had 47 undergraduates play "Mortal Kombat: Deadly Alliance" for 15 minutes. Afterward, the team took various measures of arousal, both physical and psychological. It also tested whether the students would behave more aggressively, by having them dole out hot sauce to a fellow student who, they were told, did not like spicy food but had to swallow the sauce.

Sure enough, compared with a group who had played a nonviolent video game, those who had been engaged in "Mortal Kombat" were more aggressive across the board. They gave their fellow students significantly bigger portions of the hot sauce.

Many similar studies have found the same thing: A dose of violent gaming makes people act a little more rudely than they would otherwise, at least for a few minutes after playing.

Violent Media Is One Factor

It is far harder to determine whether cumulative exposure leads to real-world hostility over the long term. Some studies in schools have found that over time digital warriors get into increasing numbers of scrapes with peers—fights in the schoolyard, for example. In a report published last summer [2012], psychologists at Brock University in Ontario found that longer periods of violent video game playing among high school students predicted a slightly higher number of such incidents over time.

"None of these extreme acts, like a school shooting, occurs because of only one risk factor; there are many factors, including feeling socially isolated, being bullied, and so on," said Craig A. Anderson, a psychologist at Iowa State University.

"But if you look at the literature, I think it's clear that violent media is one factor; it's not the largest factor, but it's also not the smallest."

Most researchers in the field agree with Dr. Anderson, but not all of them. Some studies done in schools or elsewhere have found that it is aggressive children who are the most likely to be drawn to violent video games in the first place; they are self-selected to be in more schoolyard conflicts. And some studies are not able to control for outside factors, like family situation or mood problems.

"This is a pool of research that, so far, has not been very well done," said Christopher J. Ferguson, associate professor of psychology and criminal justice at Texas A&M International University and a critic of the field whose own research has found no link. "I look at it and I can't say what it means."

Neither Dr. Ferguson, nor others interviewed in this article, receive money from the gaming industry.

The proliferation of violent video games has not coincided with spikes in youth violent crime.

Many psychologists argue that violent video games "socialize" children over time, prompting them to imitate the behavior of the game's characters, the cartoonish machismo, the hair-trigger rage, the dismissive brutality. Children also imitate flesh and blood people in their lives, of course—parents, friends, teachers, siblings—and one question that researchers have not yet answered is when, exactly, a habit is so consuming that its influence trumps the socializing effects of other major figures in a child's life.

That is, what constitutes a bad habit? In surveys about 80 percent of high school-age boys say they play video games, most of which are thought to be violent, and perhaps a third to a half of those players have had a habit of 10 hours a week or more.

The proliferation of violent video games has not coincided with spikes in youth violent crime. The number of violent youth offenders fell by more than half between 1994 and 2010, to 224 per 100,000 population, according to government statistics, while video game sales have more than doubled since 1996.

In a working paper now available online, Dr. Ward and two colleagues examined week-by-week sales data for violent video games, across a wide range of communities. Violence rates are seasonal, generally higher in summer than in winter; so are video game sales, which peak during the holidays. The researchers controlled for those trends and analyzed crime rates in the month or so after surges in sales, in communities with a high concentration of young people, like college towns.

"We found that higher rates of violent video game sales related to a decrease in crimes, and especially violent crimes," said Dr. Ward, whose co-authors were A. Scott Cunningham of Baylor University and Benjamin Engelstätter of the Center for European Economic Research in Mannheim, Germany.

No one knows for sure what these findings mean. It may be that playing video games for hours every day keeps people off the streets who would otherwise be getting into trouble. It could be that the games provide "an outlet" that satisfies violent urges in some players—a theory that many psychologists dismiss but that many players believe.

Or the two trends may be entirely unrelated.

"At the very least, parents should be aware of what's in the games their kids are playing," Dr. Anderson said, "and think of it from a socialization point of view: what kind of values, behavioral skills, and social scripts is the child learning?"

5

Violent Video Games Promote Antisocial Behaviors

Jack Flanagan

Jack Flanagan is a science and technology journalist based in London.

Panic in the media about the effects of violent video games on children is often dismissed. Nonetheless, new studies are finding that young minds are affected by these games. In one study, participants who played "nice" games were less competitive and more helpful than those who played violent games. Furthermore, another study demonstrated that participants picked up the traits of the video game characters they played, such as a higher tolerance of pain. Researchers, in fact, concluded that video games are associated with problems ranging from drug use to poor relationships. Just as nice games have positive effects, violent games are linked to negative behaviors.

Media-driven panics about what video games are "doing to our children" are scoffed at by gamers and most technology journalists. But are these haughty dismissals justified? Because studies are now coming thick and fast that find the minds of young people playing video games *are* affected by what they play. And not always for the best.

In a study titled *Remain Calm, Be Kind*, a quote from US general Colin Powell, researchers [Jodi L.] Whitaker and [Brad J.] Bushman made the point that, of all media, video games are the most perfectly architected to change our state of mind. They're active: Gamers are indirectly doing things that they'd otherwise imagine or witness in books or film respectively.

They call this "managing our mood states," implying that aggressive actions make us feel short-tempered, while slower-paced games will cause us to feel relaxed.

They set out to demonstrate this. There is a wealth of information that ties aggressive video games to anti-social behaviour. But they wanted to complete the circle: To show that "nice" games make for nicer people too. If we had this information, it would suggest that the link between game and gamer is a strong one and can be both positive and negative.

They gave participants a selection of games to play—violent, neutral and relaxing—and then asked them to compete against each other in competitive games. Those who played high-stakes gaming like *Resident Evil* were more competitive than those that played less intense games like fishing.

Players of violent games have better top-down control of their emotions. Put more plainly: They lack empathy.

Nice Games Make You Nicer

The second part was asking the participants to help sharpen pencils. They didn't know that the experiment wasn't over, so they'd be acting entirely genuinely. They found that significantly more "relaxing" gamers helped out with this trivial task than violent ones, and summarized by saying that this was the first study to ever establish that nice video games make you a nicer person.

So far, so good. We already know that violent video games make violent people. They also apparently tend to push people into more "dangerous lifestyles": Drugs, wild sex. Not the typical image of your average gamer, granted. But the question is why and how these things happen. A relationship between video games and real-life violence is not damning evidence in itself.

In another study, a group of researchers looked at reactions to faces in pain for gamers, while they lay in fMRI machines. An fMRI machine works by detecting the movement of blood around the brain, and thus what areas are being used at what times (it stands for "functional" Magnetic Resonance Imaging).

What the researchers wanted to know was how the processing of emotions was affected by a lot of video gaming, so they watched the action happening in the frontal lobes of the brains as their subjects looked at the pictures.

They found that the gamers—who all play *Counter-Strike*, a *Call of Duty*-type war game—responded less to images of real violence than non-gamers. Images of accidents and disfigured faces did not trigger the same neuro-chemical reactions as for other people.

The researchers concluded by saying players of violent games have better top-down control of their emotions. Put more plainly: They lack empathy.

A Lack of Empathy?

That certainly echoes the worries of parent and teacher groups. Although, two caveats spring to mind: Gamers might well not react to disfigured faces as much, but that might not mean they lack empathy. A lot of people began to lose touch with the image of starving children in NSPCCC [National Society for the Prevention of Cruelty to Children] adverts—which doesn't make them monsters, they've just seen the image a few times before.

And the second thing to bear in mind is that fMRI has "worked" on a dead fish. That's not to discredit the study, but it does put the results in slight perspective.

There is a hook in the study, though: The idea of BIS, our Behavioural Inhibition System. This system allows us to react better in uncertain—often violent—situations. In a war zone, when bullets are flying over your head and have been for several weeks, the last thing you want is the constant recognition of the brutality of warfare.

Similarly, in war games, to be surprised by every act of violence will get you killed. We inhibit these typically empathetic behaviors because, frankly, we have to.

The study goes on to suggest that maybe that's how we can classify those who play first-person shooters: By a "habituated" BIS circuit, or a lack of empathy to the point it isn't mandatory. They found that the part of the brain associated with empathy, the lateral prefrontal cortex, are used less in experienced gamers.

This might be active inhibition of empathy for the sake of winning the game. In-game situations are often made more intense by pleas for mercy or kindness which frequently have to be ignored.

Immersive vs. Nonimmersive

What does this mean outside of the game? It's not like fictional violence is the invention of video games. Why, German folk tales have been preaching the virtue of a messy punishment for centuries. And then there's the bible—which has been mandatory reading for billions of people.

But video games differ from these media crucially because we're not just being asked to listen and take part passively. Even as storytellers, we are playing the part of a narrator, not a performer. In video games we—everyone—is an actor. And we have to follow the script we're given.

There's another study, *Virtually Numbed*, published this year [2014], which tasked video gamers with an endurance test. They had to pick up paperclips out of a bucket of ice cold water either after reporting that they were avid gamers or actually playing a video game. Instead of looking at good vs bad, though, the researchers were interested in immersive vs non-immersive.

[Researchers] found video games correlated with every-thing from drug use to poor romantic relationships.

The researchers wanted to see what the effect was of putting yourself in the place of an automaton—i.e., a video game character that did not display emotions. They found that those people who did this were more tolerant to pain than those that didn't. They tested the hypothesis with other experiments and the conclusion was that players act similar in real life to the robotic avatars they play.

It's not just searching for good vs evil, or picking up the traits of characters you enjoy playing as. The mere act of pretending to be a virtual character can change self-perception—even down to the way we perceive physical sensation. Video games can, rather quickly, change you.

There's another paper, from 2009, with the ominous title *More Than Just a Game* that does literally think about "the children." Because childhood and the teenage years are such important parts of growing up, it's important to see what they're interacting with during that time.

Video Games Mean Trouble

The researchers took a dim view of video games. In fact, they found video games correlated with everything from drug use to poor romantic relationships. And while some of this is unsubstantiated, plenty of it is backed by their evidence, in the form of university questionnaires, and the decade of research that's come before them.

"Video games mean trouble" is the message that seems to come through in all of this. It's jumping the gun, sure, given what we know now about the benefits of relaxing video games.

But while some video games have a positive effect on mood, the ones that do, such as *Endless Ocean*, make up a negligible market share compared to big sellers such as *World of Warcraft* and *Call of Duty*, both of which are stacked with blood and death.

The psychology of all this isn't uplifting: Violent video games are linked to real-world violence, and we should stop pretending otherwise. That link is blurred, but in terms of neurochemistry there is now research that confirms that the brains of gamers change depending on what they do in-game.

In the game *Knights of the Old Republic*, a classic Star Wars spin-off, gamers can select whether to act like the "good" Jedi or the "evil" Sith. Sitting at your console, it might be hard to believe that what you do next might actually impact who you become in the real world. But it turns out the Dark Side is very real.

6

Video Game Culture Does Not Promote Antisocial Behaviors

Andrew Leonard

Andrew Leonard is a technology reporter, editor, blogger, and staff writer at Salon.

The most violent video games reflect a cesspool of sexist, racist, and brutal tendencies, creating feelings of shame among some players. At the same time, however, gaming as a culture cannot be reduced to hate and violence. Video games have a complex interrelationship with the wider culture, beyond the negative behaviors of young men. Social gaming is on the rise, and the demographics of players are becoming more similar to society in general. Also, games that encourage collaboration and community involvement are a significant part of gaming and must be acknowledged. With the availability of video games on phones, tablets, and computers, gaming is becoming commonplace and will overtake the niche of hardcore gaming.

On the other side of my desk, a Razer Blade gaming laptop is singing that siren song I know so well. *Play with me.* Sleek and stylish, the Blade is heftier than a MacBook Air, but not by much. Accompanying promotional material promises that "the world's thinnest gaming laptop" delivers the most powerful "performance in its class" (think fast-jabbing welterweight, perhaps, as opposed to heavyweight big iron).

Andrew Leonard, "'Grand Theft Auto V': Gaming's Dark Misogynist Cesspool," *Salon,* October 4, 2013. This article first appeared in Salon.com, at http://www.Salon.com. An online version remains in the Salon archives. Reprinted with permission.

The Blade boasts good specs. The Intel processor is fast, the Nvidia graphics card is stout. Reviews have been mostly positive, though some critics have dinged it for its price ($1,799 for a Windows laptop that starts with only a 128 gigabyte solid state drive is a little steep) and the not quite state-of-the-art display. But the critic who lives in my house, my 15-year-old gamer son, has pushed the machine to its limits for two weeks and pronounced himself satisfied.

Too satisfied. He mourns the fact that the Blade was provided to me for review purposes, and must be returned. I understand the feeling. While he's off at school, my fingers itch at the sight of the Blade's green backlit keyboard. Take me for a spin, the Blade whispers. You know you want to.

> *Video gaming culture should not, cannot, be reduced to young men screaming profanities as they play "Grand Theft Auto V" on their dedicated consoles.*

Solitary Play and Internalized Shame

I do, and I don't. As I contemplate the Blade, I can't get a sentence from a recent essay about the state of gaming culture out of my head. In "Poison Tree: A Letter to [video game character] Niko Bellic About Grand Theft Auto V," Tom Bissell, a writer whose gaming criticism I've read and enjoyed for years, recounts a crisis of faith in the guise of a missive addressed to "GTA V's" violence-prone, car-jacking-crazy protagonist. Although Bissell appreciates the masterly quality of "GTA V's" gameplay (ratified by the market to the tune of $1 billion in sales in just three days), his hours riding through the mean streets of Los Angeles have sparked an impressive outbreak of self-loathing.

> Solitary play can feel especially shameful, and we gamers have internalized that vaguely masturbatory shame, even those of us who've decided that solitary play can be profoundly meaningful. Niko, I've thought about this a lot, and

internalized residual shame is the best explanation I have to account for the cesspool of negativity that sits stagnating at the center of video-game culture, which right now seems worse than it's ever been.

I kind of know what Bissell is talking about. I am familiar with cesspool, reflective of so much of the Internet's worst misogynist, homophobic and racist tendencies. That "internalized residual shame" is one reason why I personally gave up gaming. Solitary play, hacking and slashing, mowing down opponents in a rage of slaughter, just didn't seem physically or mentally healthy. So I packed it in. Now I worry about what all the time my son spends gaming might be doing to him. Hell, I worry about what a *generation* growing up on ubiquitous, amazingly immersive gaming will do to the culture at large. *Something*, surely? A billion dollars was just spent in three days on a game whose structure encourages random violence and brutality. That can't be good.

And yet, at the same time, I don't know what Bissell is talking about at all. Video gaming culture should not, cannot, be reduced to young men screaming profanities as they play "Grand Theft Auto V" on their dedicated consoles. Gaming, today, encompasses much, much more. My son and his friends spend hours in the cooperative, creative world-building domain of "Minecraft" or chuckling their way through humor-drenched indie games like "Don't Starve" ("An uncompromising wilderness survival game full of science and magic"). More broadly, the explosion of mobile and social gaming has sucked all genders and ages into the gaming domain. Increasingly, it seems weird to even talk about "gaming culture." It's *the culture*, period, and we're becoming more sophisticated in how we think about and navigate it by the minute. Yes, there are cesspools. But they can be avoided.

Gaming as a Narrative Vehicle

I am watching my son and his best friend watch two actors onstage in San Francisco in a play called "The Video Game

Monologues." The scene is set in a subway car. A young man is surreptitiously eyeing a young woman beside him while she plays a game on her phone. He is delighted to see that she is playing one of his favorite games, a gothic-styled world-creation game called "Dark Manor." He's trying to work up the courage to speak to her, but wrestling with whether any overture might be rejected as intrusive or creepy. Until the very last moment, the tension builds.

The monologue is sweet and funny—a mobile-game-inflected twist on a classic moment of how-to-break-the-ice angst. We've all been there. I was struck by how obviously and intimately it spoke to the teenagers I had brought to the play. On the one hand, they were intrigued by the game; after the play, they told me it sounded like something they would like to play. But they also caught the plot. My son's friend immediately saw himself in the place of the shy young man, incredibly knowledgeable about games but extraordinarily tentative in matters of romance. He bought the narrative like a fish accepts water.

Written and directed by a woman, Lian Amaris, "The Video Game Monologues" is a slyly perceptive set of discourses on relationships embedded in gaming culture. As far as gaming cred goes, cameos by "Halo," "Words With Friends," "Dance Dance Revolution" and "Portal" were deemed "totally legit" by my son. But the games were not the action. Amaris' clear intent was to use gaming as a narrative vehicle to show how our new digital ways of play plug into the oldest stories that we've always told about each other.

So there was a meditation on aging in the form of a preschooler playing shark games on her tablet with her nursing-home grandmother. There was a father bemoaning his failure to pay proper attention to his first-person-shooter-addicted son, who has apparently committed some horrific act of mass murder. There was a girlfriend struggling not to over-kibbitz her boyfriend's stumble through some Super-Mario-like labyrinth. There may have been some cesspools lurking in the distance, but overall, the vibe was positive and affirming; a demonstration of how our life with games has real meaning.

Reducing the state of gaming culture to "Grand Theft Auto V" . . . would be like choosing one book, or one movie, to define the state of literature or film.

As such, "The Video Game Monologues" could be accused of not perfectly reflecting current reality. When I spoke to Amaris the day after the show, she acknowledged that "The Video Game Monologues" "is not a true ethnography."

"It's obviously a collection of realistic and magical fictions," said Amaris, who has master's degrees in both Performance Studies and Interactive Telecommunications. "As a show, it is designed to create a different perspective on the gaming experience and what's possible."

Reducing the state of gaming culture to "Grand Theft Auto V," said Amaris, would be like choosing one book, or one movie, to define the state of literature or film. But gaming culture, in toto, is a fast-moving, broadly sprawling target.

"People have been worried about the moral and ethical decline of video games for a long time," said Amaris, "but the mobile game boom is redefining what gamers are and what gaming culture is and it is changing old stereotypes. The kinds of gaming experiences that are out there are so varied and appeal to so many different audiences. It's a vastly different landscape than you had just a few years ago."

The most recent statistics available from the Entertainment Software Association back Amaris up. As the relative percentage of console and PC gamers has declined, mobile and social gaming has shot up—and the gender and age breakdown of gamers has become more similar to society's demographics at large. Fifty-five percent of gamers are still men, but as a percentage of all gamers, there are more women 18 and older playing games than there are men 17 and younger.

Which makes gaming culture's interrelationship with the culture more complicated than unsightly displays of bad behavior by young men would suggest.

"I genuinely believe that video games are important cultural artifacts that can help define the content of our character, just as much as exposure to a book or a movie," says Amaris, who has a day job as director of user engagement for Glu Mobile, a mobile gaming company. "In my own art and research I use video games as barometers of a sexist, racist or violent culture, always mindful that they are not the cause but the symptom."

But Amaris' art goes further. By using the language of games to talk about the human condition, Amaris brings gamers into the larger conversation, and collapses the boundaries that we set up between ourselves and those "others" who might be addicted to "Halo," or "GTA V" or "Angry Birds," or something completely different, like "Minecraft." New generations reared in an always-on, ubiquitous gaming environment will create and interpret their culture using gaming itself as a text. "The Video Game Monologues" is just a taste of what is to come.

A Collaborative Ecosystem

I am watching my son play "Minecraft," something he has done on and off for almost three years now. How does one best describe "Minecraft"? One popular shorthand is to think of it as kind of online Lego—a set of tools for building worlds made out of digital blocks. (This metaphor, however, has been complicated by the fact that in 2012 Lego started selling actual physically embodied Minecraft sets.) But you also have to imagine that the creators of Lego decided from the outset that anybody could design their own blocks and imbue them with any kind of special properties or powers that they could imagine, and then be encouraged to add those "mods" directly to the game. A critical part of "Minecraft"'s enduring popularity is its openness to community involvement. Players are participants at many levels, in a fashion analogous to the sharing-friendly participatory structure of open-source software.

"Minecraft" deserves to be included in any discussion of gaming culture as much as "Grand Theft Auto V."

Alex Leavitt, a Ph.D. student at the University of Southern California's Annenberg School of Communications, is researching how "the norms and the philosophies of open source software apply to the development of media and the creative industries."

"Minecraft" is one of his case studies, an example of a "collaborative ecosystem" in which "audiences and consumers are changing into co-producers with the people who are creating either the game or the software."

"Minecraft" deserves to be included in any discussion of gaming culture as much as "Grand Theft Auto V," if only for its demonstration of how being part of a community of gamers can generate as much satisfaction and enjoyment as actually playing the "game." Search for "Minecraft" on YouTube and you will find *millions* of videos dedicated to the world of "Minecraft." Tutorials, tours, play-by-play recordings of how a particular world was built—my son has spent countless hours watching others play the game or teach the game in addition to playing the game itself. To a certain extent this is his TV.

"How we look at game culture," says Leavitt, "requires looking through the lens of the game itself: its particular style, the way you interact with it and the conversations about it."

"'Minecraft' is open-ended," says Leavitt. "Your imagination is at the forefront of how you play the game. You are not forced to interact with the dialogues and discourses that 'Grand Theft Auto' literally shoves in your face, before you even play the game, just in the way it is advertised. In that sense, game culture is dictated by the game."

The platform and the mode of interaction make a big difference—something that explains why your grandmother might be willing to play a game on her iPhone while never daring to pick up an Xbox 360 game controller. So cool it with the cesspool naysaying: Games that encourage collaboration and community feed fountains of positivity.

In "A Letter to Niko," Tom Bissell laments the fact that an article written by a woman mildly critiquing "GTAV" received 20,000 mostly negative comments featuring the kind of hateful misogynist rhetoric all too common in contemporary online discourse. But why should it be surprising at all—or even depressing—that a game whose structure encourages and even rewards antisocial behavior nurtures a community that embodies similar, uh, values? So a game that targets young men and invites them to act out successfully attracts a horde of assholes! Something so predictable is hardly cause for despair, and it shouldn't serve as an indictment of video gaming culture writ large.

We're All Gamers

I'm mulling over that Razer Blade again. Just for old time's sake, I'm thinking. I could play the new Zerg campaign for "Starcraft II" that was released a few months back. Or I could splurge and buy that "Bioshock Infinite" game that seemed so interesting when it was getting heavily advertised. Or maybe I could try my own hand at "Minecraft."

But oddly, though I can appreciate how your typical 15-year-old hardcore gamer would desire a Razer Blade of his own with profound lust, to me, the machine looks a little quaint, a little obsolete. A dedicated gaming laptop? What isn't a gaming machine these days? I can play games on my phone, or on a tablet, or on any of my computers. Raw computing and graphics processing power might be important for playing the most bleeding-edge big budget new releases, but increasingly, the indie games that seem the most attractive or the mobile games that shoot up the app charts fastest are the games that put a premium on being clever or funny or interactive. The hardcore gamer is a niche, soon to be overwhelmed by a world in which, one way or another, we're all gamers. And that's all right.

7

Video Game Makers Have a Moral Obligation to Limit Game Violence

Simon Parkin

Simon Parkin is an author and video games journalist. His writings have appeared in the New Yorker, The Guardian, *and* Eurogamer.

Unlike violence in literature and film, the interactivity of video game violence turns spectators into active participants. A thoughtfully designed game can use the participatory nature of play for artistic ends, but the majority of games contain senseless, repetitive, and inconsequential violence. "Open world" games in which players can commit unstipulated acts such as mass murder, rape, or drunk driving beg the question of whether such play should be eliminated. Because such choices can be degrading to players, game makers are morally obligated to give meaning to or limit screen violence. As video games become more realistic, concerns about violent play will become more urgent, and the responsibility of game makers will intensify.

It was Vladimir Nabokov's wife, Véra who rescued the manuscript of "Lolita" from a back-yard incinerator at Cornell University. Beset by doubt over the book's subject matter, Nabokov hoped to burn the novel before it reached the public. Likewise, the American literary critic George Steiner had second thoughts on the publication of his 1981 novella, "The

Simon Parkin, "How Evil Should a Video Game Allow You to Be?" *New Yorker*, September 17, 2013. © The New Yorker Magazine/Simon Parkin/Condé Nast. Reproduced by permission.

Portage to San Cristobal of A.H.," in which Adolf Hitler survives the Second World War and is given the opportunity to defend his crimes. Steiner had the book recalled and pulped.

The question of whether—or to what extent—literature should allow readers into the minds of terrorists, murderers, and abusers both fictional and historical is one that continues to trouble authors. But if video-game creators share such qualms it hasn't stopped the production, in the course of the past forty years, of games that ask players to march in the boots of legions of despots and criminals, both petty and major. Long-time video-game players are guilty of innumerable virtual crimes, from minor indiscretions like jaywalking, in Atari's *Frogger*, and smoking indoors, in *Metal Gear Solid*, to more serious outrages like driving under the influence, in *Grand Theft Auto*; gunning down an airport filled with civilians, in *Call of Duty: Modern Warfare II*; and full-scale genocide in Sid Meier's *Civilization* series.

Much scripted violence in games is psychopathically repetitive and presented without broader commentary or consequence.

A 2011 Supreme Court ruling recognized that video games, like other forms of art and entertainment, are protected by the First Amendment as a form of speech. "For better or worse," Supreme Court Justice Antonin Scalia wrote in the decision, "our society has long regarded many depictions of killing and maiming as suitable features of popular entertainment." As such, Rockstar, the developer of *Grand Theft Auto V*, the latest entry in the long-running series, which was released today [September 17, 2013], could include a prolonged interactive depiction of torture without fear of censorship. Nevertheless, the "24"-esque scene, which requires players to rotate the game controller's sticks in order to tug out the victim's teeth with pliers, has inspired debate—not only over its artistic merit but also over whether such distressing inter-actions have any place in video games.

Active, If Virtual, Participants

Video-game violence is, like all onscreen violence, an act of play. But the medium has a unique capacity to inveigle, and even implicate, its audience through its interactivity. When we watch a violent scene in a film or read a description of vio-lence in a novel, no matter how graphic it is, we are merely spectators. In video games, whose stories are usually written in the second person singular—"you," rather than "he" or "she" or "I"—we are active, if virtual, participants. Often the game's story remains in stasis until we press the button to step off the sidewalk, light the cigarette, drunkenly turn the key in the ignition, or pull a yielding trigger. It is one thing to watch Gus Van Sant's 2003 "Elephant," a fictional film based on the 1999 Columbine High School massacre; it is quite another to inhabit the pixellated shoes of that atrocity's perpetrators, Eric Harris and Dylan Klebold, as one does in the video game *Super Columbine Massacre RPG*.

The ability to assume a role, rather than simply witness actions, is part of the medium's great (if woefully unexplored) potential, enabling us to inhabit the lives of people who don't necessarily share our beliefs, values, or systems of behavior. In the award-winning 2008 game *Braid*, for example, the player becomes a suit-wearing stalker chasing down an ex-lover. In the 2013 independent game *Papers, Please*, you play as a zeal-ous immigration inspector at a border checkpoint for a ficti-tious Eastern-bloc country, refusing entry to refugees. In the recent game *Cart Life*, you play as one of three downtrodden protagonists working a low-paying job in America. An enor-mously effective game that reflects the struggle of many people who live on the poverty line, it's essentially a fictionalized documentary that illuminates the subject in a way that is pos-sible only in a video game, compelling the player to experience the forces and choices that someone earning minimum wage struggles with. In this way, game designers, like novelists or filmmakers, can create truly transgressive works. A skillfully designed game might use this participatory perspective for artistic purposes—offering profound, affecting statements about the human condition. As in a film, this means that there's the potential for a kind of onscreen violence that is not merely permissible but valuable. Unfortunately, it's still a rarity: much scripted violence in games is psychopathically repetitive and presented without broader commentary or consequence. But the opportunity for a courageous designer is there.

"Open World" Games

In *Grand Theft Auto V*, the ambition is not only to tell a story but also to create a fully functioning social universe within a faithful depiction of a contemporary city. In addition to the core story, the player has the freedom to do whatever he or she wants, from taking part in a virtual triathlon to visiting a strip club to stealing cars. In this kind of video game, often described as an "open world" game, there is a difference between action that is required by the game in the course of the narrative and the action that is merely possible within the bounds [of] the game; this further complicates the question of whether the capacity for some types of play should be removed.

A creator has no moral obligation to his or her fictional characters. . . . But a game creator does *have a moral obligation to the player, who, having been asked to make choices, can be uniquely degraded by the experience.*

It's an issue all game makers face. They are, after all, small gods, constructing the rules and bounds of a reality. In previous *Grand Theft Auto* titles, for example, players were able to visit strip clubs, "kill" innocents and, in one notorious anecdote, pay for a prostitute and, after having sex with her, murder her to reclaim the money. In *Grand Theft Auto IV*, from 2008, which was a game set in Liberty City, a fictional approximation of New York, players could hijack a helicopter and, if they so chose, fly it into a skyscraper. These particular actions are not stipulated by the game maker—they do not advance the player toward beating the game. But the world and its logic both facilitate them.

Last month [August 2013], a user on a *Grand Theft Auto V* forum asked whether players would be able to rape women in the game. In the post, which was widely shared on social media, he wrote, "I want to have the opportunity to kidnap a woman, hostage her, put her in my basement and rape her everyday, listen to her crying, watching her tears." This is alarming but, in a game that prides itself on player-led freedom and opportunity within virtual, victimless but violent worlds, is it unreasonable? If this freedom is necessary to maintain the artifice of the world, the designer surely has a responsibility to engineer the victim's reactions in order to communicate something of the pain and damage inflicted.

A Moral Obligation to the Player

Fictional characters, whether they appear in novels, films, or video games, are never fully independent entities. They are conjured by words on a page, directions in a screenplay, or lines of programming code, existing only in imagination or on a screen. A creator has no moral obligation to his or her fictional characters, and in that sense anything is theoretically permissible in a video game. But a game creator *does* have a moral obligation to the player, who, having been asked to make choices, can be uniquely degraded by the experience. The game creator's responsibility to the player is to, in [author] Kurt Vonnegut's phrase, not waste his or her time. But it is also, when it comes to solemn screen violence, to add meaning to its inclusion.

Questions about video-game violence will gain urgency. The video-game medium curves toward realism or, as the novelist Nicholson Baker put it in the magazine, a "visual glory hallelujah." As the fidelity of our virtual worlds moves ever closer to that of our own, the moral duty of game makers arguably intensifies in kind. The guns in combat games are now brand-name weapons, the conflicts in them are often based on real wars, and each hair on a virtual soldier's head has been numbered by some wearied 3-D modeller. The go-to argument that video games are analogous to innocuous playground games of cops-and-robbers grows weaker as verisimilitude increases. The 1982 Atari 2600 game *Custer's Revenge*, in which players controlled a stick-man representation of General Custer tasked with raping a naked Native American woman tied to a pole, attracted plausible criticism. How much more repellent might the work be if rendered by contemporary technologies with their ever-more-realistic graphics?

The rise of motion control (where physical gestures replace traditional button-control inputs in video games) will, for many, accentuate those concerns. Some games now no longer merely require your mind and thumbs but also your entire body. In a hypothetical motion-controlled video-game version of "Lolita," it would be possible to inhabit the body, as well as the mind, of Humbert Humbert. A virtual sex crime might elicit a very different response if, instead of pressing a button to instigate it, you were required to mimic its pelvic thrusts and parries—even if, as in Nabokov's work, it was included to illustrate or illuminate, not titillate. But one wonders how many spouses would snatch that sort of work from the incinerator.

8

Violent Video Games Are a Form of Free Speech

Daniel Greenberg

Daniel Greenberg is an interactive screenwriter and game design consultant.

Violent video games are as deserving of constitutional protection under the First Amendment as other types of media. Unlike books or films, gameplay engages players in a dialogue and gives them the ability to respond emotionally. Some of the most profound explorations of violence and its contexts are currently found in mature-rated games; to create compelling moral choices, the player must be given the opportunity to make an immoral choice. Video games are also a form of free expression to players, and government officials are not in the position to decide which games enable expression. If violent video games are not protected, worse measures restricting games and their creation will appear. (In 2011, the US Supreme Court ruled that video games are a form of free speech.)

On Election Day [November 2, 2010], everyone in Washington will be focused on the polls. Everyone except the Supreme Court justices. They'll be busy with video games.

Tuesday is the day that the court has agreed to hear *Schwarzenegger v. EMA*, a case in which the state of California says it has the power to regulate the sale of violent video games to minors—in essence, to strip First Amendment free speech protection from video games that "lack serious literary, artistic, political, or scientific value for minors."

Since I express myself through the creation of video games, including violent ones, I'd like to know how government bureaucrats are supposed to divine the artistic value that a video game has for a 17-year-old. The man who spearheaded California's law, state Sen. Leland Yee, has not explained that. We've had no more clarity from [former] Gov. Arnold Schwarzenegger, who signed the bill into law.

Yee argues in his friend-of-the-court brief that since the government can "prohibit the sale of alcohol, tobacco, firearms, driver's licenses and pornography to minors," then "that same reasoning applies in the foundation and enactment" of his law restricting video games.

As a game developer, I am disheartened and a little perplexed to see my art and passion lumped in with cigarettes and booze.

Video games do more than enable the free speech rights of video game developers. Games—even those incorporating violence—enable a whole new medium of expression for players.

The U.S. Court of Appeals struck down the law as unconstitutional, just as other U.S. courts have struck down similar anti-video-game measures. California appealed to the Supreme Court, which surprisingly agreed to reconsider the lower court's rejection of the law.

So while everyone else is celebrating their constitutional right to vote, the Supreme Court will ask: Does the First Amendment bar a state from restricting the sale of violent video games to minors?

A Whole New Medium of Expression

It seems clear to me that violent video games deserve at least as much constitutional protection as other forms of media that would not be restricted under this law, such as violent books and violent movies. Books and movies enable free expression principally for their authors and makers. But video games do more than enable the free speech rights of video game developers. Games—even those incorporating violence—enable a whole new medium of expression for players.

Gameplay is a dialogue between a player and a game. Reading a book or watching a film can also be considered a dialogue, but the ability of the audience to respond is far more limited. Books and movies rarely alter their course based on the emotional reaction of the audience. (One exception would be those old Choose Your Own Adventure-type books, some of which I wrote before I started working on video games.)

The exploration and self-discovery available through books and movies is magnified in video games by the power of interactivity.

A new generation of games features real changes in the story based on the morality of a player's decisions. Mature-rated games such as "BioShock," "Fable 2" and "Fallout 3" go far beyond allowing players to engage in imaginary violent acts; they also give players meaningful consequences for the choices that they make. In "BioShock," the player meets genetically modified people who have been victimized by a mad ideology. The player can help the unfortunates or exploit them for genetic resources. The game's ending changes radically depending on the player's actions. In "Fallout 3," players can be kind to people or mistreat them, and the people will respond in kind. In "Fable 2," the player must make a painful choice to save his family from death or save thousands of innocent people—but not both.

In games such as these, gameplay becomes a powerful meditation on the nature of violence and the context in which it occurs. Some of the most thought-provoking game design is currently in Mature-rated games (similar to R-rated movies). This is because, in order to have a truly meaningful moral choice, the player must be allowed to make an immoral choice and live with the consequences.

And that's just in single-player mode.

The expressive potential of video games jumps exponentially when players take interactivity online. Players can cooperate with or compete against friends, acquaintances or strangers. They can create unique characters, build original worlds and tell their own stories in multiplayer online universes with a few or a few thousand of their friends.

Enabling Players' Free Expression

Video games, even the violent ones, enable players' free expression, just like musical instruments enable musicians' free expression. No one in the government is qualified to decide which games don't enable free speech, even when that speech comes from a 15-year-old. The courts settled the question of the First Amendment rights of minors long ago. Those rights are so strong that, for example, the Supreme Court ruled that school boards do not have the power to ban books from school libraries, even if students can obtain those books outside of school (*Board of Education v. Pico* in 1982). In that case, the justices said that "the right to receive ideas is a necessary predicate to the recipient's meaningful exercise of his own rights of speech, press, and political freedom," even when the recipient is a minor.

Many of the best developers are tackling new ways to increase players' in-game actions.

The people allowed to limit a minor's free speech rights are his parents or guardians. And maybe his grandparents and aunts and uncles. But not Sen. Yee and Gov. Schwarzenegger.

Most developers of video games will admit that we have barely begun to tap their vast potential to enable player creativity and free speech. In this early stage in the history of video games, the range of expression that we provide to players is too limited. We've done a good job of creating imaginative ways to attack our imaginary enemies, but we have not done nearly as thorough a job exploring all the other forms of human (and nonhuman) interaction.

Fortunately, many of the best developers are tackling new ways to increase players' in-game actions. I've seen some amazing early work in this field, from the biggest video game companies right down to one-person indie developers.

For example, the seemingly simple but emotionally complex online game "Darfur Is Dying" lets the player try to survive in a refugee camp without being killed by militias. "Infamous 2" promises a much richer, open-ended world to help or harm. In "Epic Mickey," Mickey Mouse will have the ability to misbehave.

One of my current projects is a game system that lets players shape and reshape the moral and spiritual development of the game world and the people in it by their actions and alliances.

Censorship Is Dangerous and Unnecessary

If California's law is upheld, it is likely that far more onerous measures will appear all over the country. Some stores may stop carrying Mature-rated games. Game publishers might be afraid to finance them. Developers would not know how to avoid triggering censorship because even the creators of such laws don't seem to know. The lawmakers won't tell us their criteria, and their lawyers have refused to reveal which existing games would be covered, even when asked in court.

Such censorship is not only dangerous, it's completely unnecessary. More than 80 scholars and researchers from schools such as George Mason University and Harvard Medical School have written an extensive friend-of-the-court brief in opposition to the law, noting that California failed to produce any real evidence showing that video games cause psychological harm to minors. And even if there was harm, the law's supporters have not shown that the statute could alleviate it.

The game development community has worked hard on creating a rating system that clearly discloses games' content. Even our critics, such as the Federal Trade Commission, have praised our efforts. The FTC's own survey shows that 87 percent of parents are satisfied with the rating system.

Parents have good reason to be concerned about their children's media diet and to ask what possible good can come from blowing out the brains of a character in a game. Make-believe violence appears to have many benefits for minors, such as relieving stress, releasing anger and helping children cope with difficult feelings such as powerlessness and fear of real violence. A recent Texas A&M International study shows that violent games could actually reduce violent tendencies and could be used as a therapy tool for teens and young adults.

There is no small irony that the man helping to spearhead the charge against violent video games is Schwarzenegger, the Terminator himself. He, more than anyone, should understand the thrill of a good fake explosion.

Even when video games contain graphic violence, and even when the players are minors whose parents let them play games with violence, picking up that game controller is a form of expression, and it should be free.

9

Barring Sales of Violent Games to Minors Does Not Violate Free Speech

Joseph J. Horton

Joseph J. Horton is a psychology professor at Grove City College in Pennsylvania and researcher with the Center for Vision & Values.

The US Supreme Court's 2011 decision to strike down restrictions against the sale of violent video games to people under eighteen contradicts traditions and laws that regulate the types of speech to which minors are exposed, such as barring them from attending R-rated films without an adult or buying pornography. Video games are pretend, and most kids who play them do not commit crimes or murders, but the effects of violent media—increased desensitization and aggression—are measurable. Despite the Supreme Court's disappointing decision, parents must rise to the challenge of free speech in video games and monitor what their children play.

Should a thirteen-year-old be able to purchase a school-shooting simulator without parents' knowledge or consent? The Supreme Court says that freedom of speech requires they do have that opportunity. On June 27, [2011] in a 7-2 decision, the court struck down a California law barring the sale of graphically violent video games to people under eighteen.

Joseph J. Horton, "A Free Speech Challenge for Parents," *Humanist*, September/October 2011. Copyright © 2011 by Joseph J. Horton. All rights reserved. Reproduced by permission.

I haven't seen legal minds commenting on what seem (to me) to be obvious consequences of this decision. If the First Amendment requires that minors be able to purchase graphically violent video games, does this mean minors may attend R-rated movies without an adult or purchase pornography? We have longstanding traditions and laws that regulate the speech to which minors may be exposed without the consent of their parents.

Reasons to Be Concerned

Research on the effects of violent video games has shown that parents and society have reason to be concerned. We're not talking about the games from my youth like *Space Invaders* or games that involved a cartoon-like image of a person falling over. Today's games include graphic, movie-quality images of death and dismemberment. And unlike a movie, which is viewed passively, game players are actively causing the scenes that unfold before them.

Greater exposure to violent media desensitizes people to the effects of violence and aggression.

Yes, video games are pretend. Of course, they are. Even young teenagers who play the games know they aren't real. Yet, even passively viewing pretend images affects the way people think. Television commercials are fictional, to the point of fantasy, and we all know this. The reason some of the most successful businesses in the world advertise—even paying over two-million dollars for a thirty-second Super Bowl spot—is not to generously provide free television for us but because data shows that advertising changes consumers' attitudes and behavior. Active participation, like playing a video game, changes attitudes and behavior more efficiently than passively watching TV.

Anders Behring Breivik, the man charged with killing at least seventy-six people in the recent bomb attack and summer camp shooting in Norway, writes about playing the graphically violent game *Modern Warfare 2*. To learn more about this game, I was required to enter my birth date on its website, modernwarfare2.infinityward.com. This indicates that the producers of the game recognize the content is inappropriate for children. The game is essentially a combat simulator that provides a virtual training ground for people prone to mass murder.

Will most kids who play games that simulate school shootings live out the roles they are playing? No. Will most kids who play *Grand Theft Auto* steal cars? No. Very few kids who play violent video games will perform those acts in real life. The changes most kids will experience as a result of playing violent video games are more subtle than becoming mass murderers, but are still quite measurable.

For example, greater exposure to violent media desensitizes people to the effects of violence and aggression. What would normally be abhorrent becomes "not so bad" or perhaps even funny. Violent video games cause users to think more violent thoughts. Typical behavioral effects from these changes in thinking might range from not being appropriately moved by images of real human suffering to being more argumentative and disrespectful.

Although there isn't ample space here for a full consideration of the effects of using violent video games, I can easily spend an entire class period in my course on child development discussing violent media. Among its well-established effects is that users of violent media are more likely to believe that crime victims deserved their fate. In addition, users of violent media have a distorted view of the world, believing life to be significantly less safe than it is.

It's true that people who are prone to aggressiveness are more likely to use violent media. It is also true that people who use violent media become more aggressive. None of us want to believe that we will acquire a taste for the distasteful, but if we consume enough of what began as distasteful, it becomes satisfying.

Straining the First Amendment?

Make no mistake about it; video games can be a great use of free time. Research shows that kids who play video games develop better spatial skills and hand-eye coordination. Multiplayer games can also teach social and management skills. These games are also just plain fun. Yet the benefits of video games do not require gruesome images.

We endure a lot of ugliness to protect our right to free speech. Like Justices Clarence Thomas and Steven Breyer, I do not believe that denying the sale of violent video games to people under eighteen would have strained the First Amendment. With or without laws that require adult involvement for kids to have questionable material, however, parents must be parents. Laws are no substitute for parental monitoring. While I find the Court's decision disappointing, it highlights the need for parents to be proactive and willing to make tough decisions.

10

The Video Games Rating System Is Effective

Ilya Shapiro, Thomas S. Leatherbury, John P. Elwood, and Paul B. Spelman

Ilya Shapiro is a senior fellow in constitutional studies at the Cato Institute and editor-in-chief of the Cato Supreme Court Review. *Thomas S. Leatherbury, John P. Elwood, and Paul B. Spelman are partners at Vinson & Elkins, an international law firm.*

The video game industry's self-regulatory rating system, overseen by the Entertainment Software Rating Board (ESRB), is praised for its effectiveness. The board's age-based ratings provide accurate content descriptors and summaries, with detailed information on depictions of violence, gore, and the use of alcohol and tobacco. While submitting games for rating is not a legal requirement, most game consoles will not play titles without an ESRB rating, and retailer enforcement of ratings is higher than that of the music and film industries. Moreover, the ESRB system is widely known and considered useful by adults—who use the ratings in combination with parental controls for game consoles and computers—and responsive to public concerns, continually improving its methods.

The most effective self-regulatory systems have been found to involve age-based ratings, detailed content description, and vigorous retailer enforcement. Such systems prevent mi-

Ilya Shapiro, Thomas S. Leatherbury, John P. Elwood, and Paul B. Spelman, "Brief of the Cato Institute as Amicus Curiae Supporting Respondents," Entertainment Software Association, September 2010. Copyright © 2010 by Cato Institute. All rights reserved. Reproduced by permission.

nors from accessing mature content without parental consent while providing parents with the information necessary to decide for themselves the amount of exposure that is appropriate for their children.

The video game industry already has such a system, one that incorporates the most effective attributes of other entertainment industries' self-regulatory mechanisms while avoiding those elements that can limit their impact. Respected sources (including the Federal Trade Commission) have called the video game industry's ratings and enforcement regime the most effective industry self-regulation in the entertainment field today, and it is one that is continually improving. . . .

[ESRB] game summaries have been described as a "quantum leap" forward for parental guidance.

The ESRB [Entertainment Software Rating Board] rating system incorporates the most effective attributes of the MPAA [Motion Picture Association of America] ratings while improving on that system by furnishing additional information and stronger enforcement mechanisms. The ESRB system also avoids some of the elements that have limited the impact of the music and television ratings systems. The result is a system about which the FTC has recently observed, "[o]f the three entertainment sectors, the electronic game industry continues to have the strongest self-regulatory code." Furthermore, the ESRB has continued to improve the ratings system in response to public concerns. As the FTC noted:

> the video game industry outpaces the movie and music industries in the three key areas that the Commission has been studying for the past decade: (1) restricting target-marketing of mature-rated products to children; (2) clearly and prominently disclosing rating information; and (3) restricting children's access to mature-rated products at retail. . . .

The ESRB System Provides Age Ratings, Content Descriptors, and Summaries

Much like the film and TV ratings systems, the ESRB system uses an age-based rating method, assigning every game one of the following ratings:

- EC (Early Childhood), which is suitable for ages three and over and contains no material that parents would find inappropriate;

- E (Everyone), which is for ages six and older and may contain minimal cartoon, fantasy, or mild violence and may infrequently use mild language;

- E10+ (Everyone 10+), which is for ages ten and over and may contain more cartoon, fantasy, or mild violence and mild language or minimal suggestive themes;

- T (Teen), which is for ages thirteen and older and may contain violence, suggestive themes, crude humor, minimal blood, simulated gambling, and infrequent strong language;

- M (Mature), for ages seventeen and over and which may contain intense violence, blood and gore, sexual content, and strong language;

- AO (Adults Only), which is for ages eighteen and older and may include prolonged scenes of intense violence and graphic sexual content and nudity.

In addition, the ESRB, like the MPAA system, provides detailed content descriptors, such as:

- Fantasy Violence—Violent actions of a fantasy nature, involving human or non-human characters in situations easily distinguishable from real life;

- Animated Blood—Discolored and/or unrealistic depictions of blood;

- Comic Mischief—Depictions or dialogue involving slapstick or suggestive humor;

- Simulated Gambling—Player can gamble without betting or wagering real cash or currency.

Notably, there are content descriptors for depictions of (or references to) alcohol and tobacco use, subjects on which many parents say they want information. Both the age rating and content descriptors are prominently displayed on packaging material, as well as on most video game retailer websites.

Furthermore, a more comprehensive description of game contents, the "rating summary," is available on the ESRB website, through a cell phone application, and in bimonthly parental emails. Such game summaries have been described as a "quantum leap" forward for parental guidance, offering "a level of information not provided by any of the other major media rating systems, and ... they represent an unprecedented resource for parents."

An Independent Panel Rates Nearly Every Game and the System Is Well Enforced by Retailers

Although—as with the MPAA system—game producers are not legally required to submit games for rating, game consoles made by major manufacturers are designed so that they will not play a game without an ESRB rating. As a consequence, the vast majority of video games are submitted to ESRB. Once a game is rated, a game manufacturer is "legally bound, by contract, to disclose all pertinent content."

As with the film system, ESRB's ratings are assigned by an independent panel of specially trained adult raters who are not themselves "gamers" and who "typically have experience with children through prior work experience, education or by being parents or caregivers themselves." ESRB raters review a video sample and written answers to a questionnaire submitted by the game manufacturer. The sample must contain representative content from the game, including content not meant to be accessed by players. After a rating is assigned, a manufacturer may accept the rating, refine the game's content and resubmit, or appeal to an appeals board consisting of publishers, retailers and other professionals. They can also release a game without a rating but, as noted above, the game will then not play on most game consoles.

As with the MPAA system, the ESRB system is well established and widely understood.

Following a game's release, ESRB staff and raters may follow up by playing the game to ensure that the video sample was accurate and complete. Unlike other rating systems, the ESRB can enforce the requirement of complete and accurate submissions through heavy fines (up to $1 million) and other sanctions against game manufacturers. The ESRB can also change a game's rating post-release and require the manufacturer to recall and relabel packaging and promotional materials. The ESRB has changed ratings post-release twice in recent years, and the risk of such a costly action creates a powerful deterrent to withholding information relevant to rating. The maker of *Grand Theft Auto: San Andreas* incurred some $24.5 million in recall costs when the ESRB changed the game's rating after discovering hidden mature content.

Once games are in stores, the system depends on retailers' voluntary enforcement of the ratings for any purchaser of an M-rated game who appears to be under 17. The most recent FTC study found that retailers do so roughly 80% of the time, 8% higher than theater enforcement of R-rated film restrictions, and more than 60% better than enforcement of the music industry's PAL [Parental Advisory Label] mechanism. More importantly, according to the FTC, compliance is improving, and retailers now have a "robust system" in place "[t]o assist parents in their gate-keeping role."

The ESRB system is the most comprehensive, effective, and responsive parental guidance system in the entertainment field today.

The ESRB System Is Widely Understood, Accurate and Effective, Particularly in Combination with Parental Controls

As with the MPAA system, the ESRB system is well established and widely understood. The most recent FTC data indicate that 87% of parents are aware of the system; 73% of that number (61% of parents overall) said they review the rating most or all of the time before their child plays a video game for the first time. Awareness levels of the ESRB system have risen significantly since 2000, when only 61% of parents were aware of it. Although recognizing that "[u]niform agreement among parents about game ratings is unrealistic," the FTC found that 64% of parents familiar with the system agreed that "most or all of the time" the ratings matched their personal view of whether a game was suitable for children, and another 24% agreed with the ratings "some of the time." The FTC found that parents "generally appear to be using ESRB ratings as a decision-making tool in conjunction with their own separate monitoring of their children's game-playing habits."

The FTC has found striking consensus among parents about the utility of ESRB ratings. Sixty percent of parents familiar with the system considered it "good" or "excellent" at informing them about the level of violence in a game, and

87% reported being "very" or "somewhat" satisfied with ESRB ratings. Meanwhile, 94% of parents found the ratings "moderately" or "very" easy to understand.

In addition to point-of-purchase restrictions on sales of mature-themed games to minors, the computer and gaming industries have developed parental controls for current PC systems and major game consoles that allow parents to monitor and manage their children's game play. These controls allow parents to limit access to the Internet, limit games by ESRB age rating, and limit the amount of time the child can play. And in contrast to V-chip technology, parents appear to understand and appreciate video game parental controls. The most in-depth survey of its kind (admittedly conducted by a private survey firm on behalf of respondent ESA), which gathered data from 1,200 households nationally, found that 76% of parents found video game parental controls "useful." Microsoft, manufacturer of the Xbox game consoles, also has an ongoing public service campaign to educate parents on the use of parental controls.

The ESRB System Is Responsive to Public Concerns

While no parental guidance mechanism is immune to criticism, the ESRB, more than any other entertainment ratings system, has evolved in response to public concerns, continually refining and improving its rating system. In 2005, for instance, the ESRB added the older "Everyone" category (E10+), and changed its rules to require that video samples include content not meant to be accessed by players. The ESRB also increased its fine for misrepresenting game content to a maximum of $1 million and, in 2007, changed from part-time to full-time game raters. Then in 2008, the ESRB added the comprehensive rating summaries in order to provide parents with more information. . . .

The ESRB System Gives Control to Parents

It is evident that the video game industry is serious about giving parents control over minors' exposure to depictions of violence. The ESRB system is the most comprehensive, effective, and responsive parental guidance system in the entertainment field today. In fact, the National Institute on Media and the Family has stated that given all of the improvements to the ESRB system over the past few years, the Institute has "increasingly shifted [its] attention to the role of parents" in protecting children from age-inappropriate content.

Concerns over violence in popular entertainment and its effect on minors have been present for centuries. The appropriate response has always been industry self-regulation and parental involvement—and that is true here as well. The current ratings system effectively affords parents the ability to control their children's exposure to violence while avoiding unwarranted limitations on free expression.

The Video Games Rating System Is Not Effective

Jason Dafnis

Jason Dafnis is cofounder and editor at the Blunder Busters, an entertainment website.

The system used by the Entertainment Software Rating Board (ESRB) to rate video games is flawed. For example, its board members are not required to play the games they evaluate; watching one is an entirely different experience than playing one. The ESRB's descriptions are ineffective, and rating summaries ignore the interactive nature of games. In addition, the board largely keeps its rating processes and who rates the games secret. Finally, the ESRB's rating standards are not standardized, having developed a streamlined approach in which the board may not view some content of games at all. While its system still functions as a guide for the appropriateness of games, the ESRB must reform its policies.

W e take it for granted-but *should* we?

Everyone knows that the Entertainment Software Rating Board [ESRB] is an objective, sensible reference tool with which gamers can make informed decisions about what games to play based on the appropriateness of their content. But what you *don't* know is that it's a fatally flawed system that does more harm than good for the gaming community and the industry at large. Here's a concise look at why.

ESRB Board Members Don't Actually Play the Games They Rate

When you go see a movie, you rightly assume that the "PG-13" or "R" rating that movie holds was assigned by people who had actually watched the same movie you're about to see. Naturally, this is a standard of the MPAA [Motion Picture Association of America]: the rater must watch the film as it will be distributed and rate it accordingly. Unfortunately, the ESRB doesn't see it that way and doesn't require their rating board to play the video games they rate.

The essential difference between video games and other media—interactivity—necessitates a better way to classify their content.

Instead, the ESRB requires game publishers to submit two types of materials in lieu of the gaming experience. Those two materials are from the ESRB website:

1. *a completed ESRB online questionnaire detailing the game's pertinent content [being content the developer deems most extreme—ed.], which essentially translates to anything that may factor into the game's rating. This includes not only the content itself (violence, sexual content, language, controlled substances, gambling, etc.), but other relevant factors such as context, reward systems and the degree of player control; and*

2. *a DVD that captures all pertinent content, including typical gameplay, missions, and cutscenes, along with the most extreme instances of content across all relevant categories.*

> *Pertinent content that is not playable (i.e., "locked out")*
> *but will exist in the game code on the final game disc*
> *must also be disclosed*

The excuse is that some games can be very long and that every player will experience the game differently, making it impractical for board members to scour a game like *Skyrim* for every instance of suggestive content. But there are several aspects overlooked here, chiefly among them the differences between *watching* a video game and *playing* one. In fact, the only time an ESRB rater might play-test a game they've rated is once it's been released.

Even if context and perspective are taken into account, watching footage of the "extreme" parts of a game is like reading the screenplays of every sex scene in *Game of Thrones* without knowing what's going on around them. The essential difference between video games and other media—interactivity—necessitates a better way to classify their content. In the same way the MPAA wouldn't send a harlequin-reading soccer mom to rate *Oldboy*, the ESRB needs to dedicate knowledgeable gamers to their ratings boards. Which they don't.

> *While they are not required to have advanced skills as video*
> *game players, . . . [ESRB raters] often gain or further develop*
> *such abilities. . . .*
>
> *ESRB FAQ webpage*

ESRB Descriptions Are Poorly Framed

On a typical ESRB rating, you might expect to see content descriptors like "Blood and Gore," "Strong Language," and, most vaguely, "Suggestive Content." These serve their purpose well enough, even if they're often inaccurate (especially in the GameCube/Xbox/PS2 era) and not particularly informative. But a closer look at the long-form descriptions reveals their ineffectiveness.

Recently, the ESRB posted one such "Rating Summary" for the upcoming *Metal Gear Solid: Ground Zeroes*. Here are some excerpts.

> *"Players infiltrate various bases and use pistols, machine guns, and rocket launchers to kill enemy soldiers. . . ."*

> *"Players can also employ stealth attacks (e.g., choking, knife stabbing from behind) and have the ability to kill non-adversary characters/prisoners."*

> *"The words "f**k" and "sh*t" are heard in the dialogue."*

On the surface, these are objective concerns that might be relevant to a gamer's desire to play the game. But anybody who's played a *Metal Gear Solid* game knows that "employing stealth attacks" and hearing expletives aren't the main attractions of the game—but the framing of the rating summary makes it sound like that's the whole game.

Sweeping stories, engaging mechanics, and awesome visuals are just a few of many factors that drive us to play video games like *Metal Gear Solid*. It comes back to that simple fact: the ESRB directly ignores the nature of video games as an interactive medium. And it's due to that ignorance that the rating summary's epistemological potential is really wasted.

On top of the fact that ESRB raters don't play the games, they now don't even need to see for themselves even some of the game's content.

The ESRB Keeps It Creepily Clandestine

Maybe this one isn't necessarily the presence of something bad, but the absence of something good. The ESRB's processes, while partially disclosed through FAQs [frequently asked questions] and informative materials, are largely unknown to the general public. Moreover, there's no known figurehead or PR [public relations] specialist to maintain a public presence—and the black-and-white rating logo is a depressing mascot for any organization appealing itself to gamers.

Moreover, individual raters are kept anonymous and are rarely known to the press, opting instead to be ghosts without voices. Really, the image we get is that of jury members rather than video game content raters.

ESRB's Rating Standards Aren't Standard

According to the ESRB's FAQ page, there are two processes by which games are rated today. The first, more traditional method involves raters reviewing submissions and assigning ratings as appropriate. That method is and has been used to rate "all packaged or boxed games sold at retail"—e.g., the games you can pick up from GameStop or Wal-Mart. However, due to the prolific digital-distribution industry, the ESRB has developed a "streamlined" (read: lax) method for rating digitally distributed games and apps.

> *"This streamlined process utilizes a different online questionnaire with multiple-choice questions relating to various categories of pertinent content (violence, language, sexuality, substances, etc.), context and other features (the player's perspective, the game's realism and reward system, etc.). Once the developer or publisher completes the questionnaire, the combination of responses provided immediately and automatically generates a rating for that game or app."*

While I wasn't able to get a hold of this questionnaire, that wording certainly implies a minimum of human judgment and response when assigning a rating. On top of the fact that ESRB raters don't play the games, they now don't even need to see for themselves even some of the game's content. Even though they take retaliatory action against shifty publishers and developers, shame on the ESRB for their inconsistency in knowing the products they rate.

The Entertainment Software Ratings Board might not be public enemy number one in the game industry, but it's certainly amiss in its duties and execution. They sit on uncomfortable ground, being not legally mandated (for rating application or age-restricted sale) but almost universally implemented. While their ratings still serve as a guide for appropriateness for younger audiences, the ESRB needs to reform its rating policies, starting with raters themselves. Gamers need—in fact, they *deserve*—a more *gamer*-friendly policy.

Organizations to Contact

The editors have compiled the following list of organizations concerned with the issues debated in this book. The descriptions are derived from materials provided by the organizations. All have publications or information available for interested readers. The list was compiled on the date of publication of the present volume; the information provided here may change. Be aware that many organizations take several weeks or longer to respond to inquiries, so allow as much time as possible.

American Psychological Association (APA)
750 First St. NE, Washington, DC   20002-4242
(800) 374-2721
website: www.apa.org

The mission of the American Psychological Association (APA) is to "advance psychology as a science, as a profession, and as a means of promoting human welfare." As part of its commitment to social welfare, the APA investigates the potential link between violent video games and increased aggression in children. Its website includes information and reports on video games and the impacts of gaming, including *Video Games: Old Fears and New Directions*, a special issue of the APA's journal *Review of General Psychology*.

Common Sense Media
650 Townsend, Suite 435, San Francisco, CA   94103
(415) 863-0600 • fax: (415) 863-0601
website: www.commonsensemedia.org

Common Sense Media is a nonprofit, nonpartisan organization with a mission of providing kids and families with information on media and technology. The group provides ratings of video games, websites, and music, among other forms of media, and offers articles for parents, educators, and kids. It also maintains blogs for parents and educators.

EdgeGamers® Organization (eGO)
website: www.edge-gamers.com

EdgeGamers® Organization is dedicated to providing a safe place for gamers from all over the world to meet for family-friendly and respectful game play. Participants must follow a strict code of conduct that bans racist, political, and degrading speech. The organization's website offers an arcade, competitions, player blogs, news, and forums.

Entertainment Software Association (ESA)
575 7th St. NW, Suite 300, Washington, DC   20004
e-mail: esa@theesa.com
website: www.theesa.com

The Entertainment Software Association (ESA) is a US association exclusively dedicated to serving the business and public affairs needs of video game companies. Its website offers comprehensive sections dedicated to public policy, industry facts, and parent resources, as well as a news room.

Entertainment Software Rating Board (ESRB)
317 Madison Ave., 22nd Floor, New York, NY   10017
website: www.esrb.org

Established in 1994, the Entertainment Software Rating Board (ESRB) is a nonprofit regulatory agency created by the Entertainment Software Association. The board rates video games based on content and the targeted age group. Game-specific ratings are available on its website, which also contains information pages on recent industry news, parent and consumer protection, and education and outreach programs.

International Game Developers Association (IGDA)
19 Mantua Rd., Mt. Royal, NJ   08061
(856) 423-2990 • fax: (856) 423-3420
website: www.igda.org

International Game Developers Association (IGDA) is an industry association that promotes career development and fosters community interests within the field of video game design. Part of the IGDA mission is to fight censorship of video games. Online, the association offers numerous position papers on concerns over video game rating and censorship. It also publishes a newsletter, *Perspectives*.

Parents' Choice Foundation

201 West Padonia Rd., Suite 303, Timonium, MD   21093
(410) 308-3858 • fax: (410) 308-3877
e-mail: info@parents-choice.org
website: www.parents-choice.org

The Parents' Choice Foundation is the nation's oldest non-profit media guide for children's toys and media. Reviews are provided by grandparents, parents, children, teachers, librarians, writers, and artists. In addition, Parents' Choice publishes a monthly e-newsletter.

Video Game Voters Network (VGVN)

website: www.videogamevoters.org

Video Game Voters Network (VGVN) works to organize gamers against threats to video games. The network provides news on video game legislation, encourages its members to register to vote, and suggests ways for members to take action. VGVN opposes efforts to regulate the content of entertainment media, including proposals to criminalize the sale of certain games to minors or regulate video games differently from movies, music, books, and other media.

Bibliography

Books

Tom Bissell

Extra Lives: Why Video Games Matter. New York: Pantheon Books, 2010.

Drew Davidson, ed.

Well Played 3.0: Video Games, Value, and Meaning. Pittsburgh, PA: ETC Press, 2011.

Dave Grossman and Gloria DeGaetano

Stop Teaching Our Kids to Kill: A Call to Action Against TV, Movie, and Video Game Violence. New York: Harmony Books, 2014.

Joseph Kahne, Ellen Middaugh, and Chris Evans

The Civic Potential of Video Games. Cambridge, MA: MIT Press, 2009.

Steven J. Kirsh

Children, Adolescents, and Media Violence: A Critical Look at the Research, 2nd ed. Thousand Oaks, CA: SAGE Publications, 2012.

Lawrence Kutner and Cheryl K. Olson

Grand Theft Childhood: The Surprising Truth About Violent Video Games and What Parents Can Do. New York: Simon & Schuster, 2008.

Liel Leibovitz

God in the Machine: Video Games as Spiritual Pursuit. West Conshohocken, PA: Templeton Press, 2014.

Jane McGonigal   *Reality Is Broken: Why Games Make Us Better and How They Can Change the World*. New York: Penguin Press, 2011.

Chris Melissinos and Patrick O'Rourke   *The Art of Video Games: From Pac-Man to Mass Effect*. New York: Welcome Books, 2013.

Brooke Strickland and Andrew Doan   *Hooked on Games: The Lure and Cost of Video Game and Internet Addiction*. Coralville, IA: F.E.P. International, 2012.

Periodicals and Internet Sources

Tom Chick   "Speaking the Unspoken Truth About Gender Inequality in Videogames," Quarter to Three, November 27, 2013. www.quartertothree.com.

Christian de Luna   "Guns and Games: On the Possibility of Using Video Games to Teach About Gun Safety and Trauma," *Momentum*, vol. 1, no. 1, 2012.

Entertainment Software Association   "Essential Facts About Games and Violence," 2013. www.theesa.com.

Jeff Grabmeier   "Denied the Chance to Cheat or Steal, People Turn to Violent Video Games," Ohio State University, March 12, 2013. http://researchnews.osu.edu.

John M. Grohol   "Violence & Video Games: A Weak, Meaningless Correlation," PsychCentral, September 18, 2013. http://psychcentral.com/blog.

Doug Gross   "10 Most Controversial Violent Video Games," CNN, August 26, 2013. www.cnn.com.

Tom Higgins   "Grand Theft Auto V Is Designed Deliberately to Degrade Women," *Telegraph*, October 4, 2013.

James Lileks   "Put Down the Controller!," *National Review*, March 11, 2013.

Randy Pitchford and Dave Grossman   "Point . . . Counterpoint: Do Videogames Inspire Violent Behavior? Absolutely Not, Says Vidgame Developer Randy Pitchford. Absolutely Yes, Says Lt. Col. David Grossman," *Variety*, Winter 2013.

Gabe Rottman   "Worse Facts Make Worst Law with Violent Video Games," *Free Future*, December 20, 2012. www.aclu.org/blog.

Andrew L. Schlafly   "Game Over for Childhood? Violent Video Games as First Amendment Speech," *Rutgers Computer & Technology Law Journal*, Fall 2012.

Jordan Shapiro   "Violent Video Games Can Turn Kids into Progressive Intellectuals," *Forbes*, February 9, 2014.

Beth Teitell   "Violent Video Games Put Parental
                        Judgment to Test," *Boston Globe*,
                        January 7, 2013.

Patrick Thomas   "5 Ways Video Games Are Saving
and Rich   Mankind," Cracked, April 13, 2013.
Solomon   www.cracked.com.

Mark Walsh   "Mortal Combat: Video Game
                        Makers Fight for Their Right to Be
                        as Bad as They Wanna Be," *ABA
                        Journal*, November 2010.

Gail Wood   "Evil or Benign? Video Games Need
                        Parental Monitoring," *Charisma
                        News*, April 4, 2013. www
                        .charismanews.com.

Index

Resident Evil (video game), 45
Rockefeller, Jay, 31

S

Sandy Hook Elementary School,
  11, 26, 31
Sarkeesian, Anita, 8
Scarborough, Joe, 31
Schwarzenegger, Arnold, 66, 68
Schwarzenegger v. EMA (2010),
  65–66
Science, technology, engineering,
  and mathematics (STEM), 13
Sexism in video games, 7–8, 27,
  55
Shapiro, Ilya, 75–82
Shooter video games
  benefits of, 12–13
  cognitive performance and, 14
  player becomes shooter, 24–25
Simulated Gambling rating, 78
Social benefits of gaming, 19–21
Social networking games, 19
South Korea, 34
Spatial skills of gamers, 13, 14, 74
Spelman, Paul B., 75–82
Splatterhouse (video game), 31
Steiner, George, 59–60
Sweet spot in motivation, 16

T

Texas A&M International, 70
Texas A&M International Univer-
  sity, 34, 42
Thomas, Clarence, 74
Tomb Raider (video game), 7
T (Teen) rating, 77
Trump, Donald, 30–31

U

University of Georgia, 32
University of Southern California,
  56
University of Texas, 40

V

V-chip technology, 81
Video game makers
  gamers and, 61–62
  in-game actions, 68–69
  moral obligation of, 63–64
  open world games, 62–63
  overview, 59–61
The Video Game Monologues
  (Amaris), 53–55
Violent media, 41–43
Violent video games
  antisocial behavior and, 44–49
  benefit for children, 10–21
  claims of violence, 30–31
  crime rates and, 39–43
  desensitization and aggression
    with, 22–28
  do not cause violence, 29–38
  free speech rights of, 65–70
  government action against, 31
  gun violence concerns, 31,
    34–35, 37
  industry reaction to, 36
  introduction, 7–9
  mass shooters and, 35–36
  overview, 10–12, 29–30, 39–40
  player demographics, 32
  regulation of, 36–37
  research on, 32–34, 40–41
  as scapegoat, 37–38
  sexism in, 7–8, 27, 55